MIMESIS
INTERNATIONAL

PHILOSOPHY
n. 21

Joseph Margolis

THREE PARADOXES OF PERSONHOOD: THE VENETIAN LECTURES

Edited by
Roberta Dreon

 MIMESIS

© 2017 – MIMESIS INTERNATIONAL
www.mimesisinternational.com
e-mail: info@mimesisinternational.com

Isbn: 9788869771040
Book series: *Philosophy,* n. 21

© MIM Edizioni Srl
P.I. C.F. 02419370305

TABLE OF CONTENTS

Joce — 6.6.16.

satire +
esoteric theme +
wider attack on Rationalism in our time

Sketches by kind concession of Jale N. Erzen

ROBERTA DREON

ON JOSEPH MARGOLIS' PHILOSOPHY.
AN INTRODUCTION

> I've been aware for a good many years that all my inquiries,
> no matter how scattered, have been converging with increasing
> insistence on the definition of the human self and the analysis of
> the unique features of the human world and our form of life. And
> yet, for all its plausibility, what I find to be its immense importance
> remains largely ignored in the academic literature.[1]

It could be said that Joseph Margolis' intellectual profile is the result of
a narrative that does not belong to a single philosophical tradition. He was
and still is capable of crossing and even ironically criticizing the boundaries
between analytic philosophy, continental philosophy and pragmatism,
although he is well-acquainted not only with the subjects and methods
characterizing each philosophical tradition, but also, I would argue, with
the habits ruling each theoretical form of life, its language and even its
sometimes almost idiosyncratic dialect.

Margolis was originally trained in analytic philosophy, even though
he caught the last glimmers of pragmatism at Columbia University in
the late 1940s. While pragmatism soon came to be perceived as a thing
of the past, analytic philosophy seemed to offer the only viable chance
to rigorously practice philosophy in the U.S. in the 1950s and 1960s.
However, as Margolis himself declared, he began to feel that he was
restricting himself "in the same way the analytic philosophers were"[2] and
turned to study continental philosophy, particularly phenomenology —
both Husserl's orthodoxy and Heidegger's very different approach —
with a peculiar interest in the detranscendentalizing efforts of Maurice
Merleau-Ponty.

---

1   Joseph Margolis, *Towards a Metaphysics of Culture*, in Dirk-Martin Grube,
     Robert Sinclair (ed.), *Pragmatism, Metaphysics and Culture. Reflextions on the
     Philosophy of Joseph Margolis* (Helsinki: Nordic Pragmatism Network, 2015), p.
     1.
2   Joseph Margolis, 'Interview with Joseph Margolis', *European Journal for
     Pragmatism and American Philosophy*, VI/1 (2014), p. 309.

His return to pragmatism took place rather late, in the 1980s, and was essentially related to the intrinsic development of his own thought,[3] rather than to the trend of the moment, which was due to the innovative move by Richard Rorty and then further developed by his engagement with Hilary Putnam's new version of pragmatism.

Nonetheless, seen from the current point of view, Margolis' intellectual path has something to share with his beloved philosophical hero, the Hegel of the *Phenomenology of the Spirit*. This is not to say that he was pursuing a kind of up-to-date metaphysical system; rather, today the sort of convergence he mentions in the above quotation has become quite evident. It seems as though his wide range of interests in the aesthetic, ontological, and epistemological fields over his long career are now flowing into a naturalistic anthropology of the distinctively human emergence — a metaphysics of culture that must be basically interpreted as the two sides of the same process. Given Margolis' strong criticism of any kind of methodological individualism, no history of the "spirit" — even in its radically immanent, contingent, and naturalistic version — can be developed apart from the human world in its complexity. At the same time, each moment of this heterodox phenomenology maintains its value in the multifaceted picture of a completely contingent, provisional and still open history.

The *Venetian Lectures* we are going to present here in their revised literary form can be considered a succinct yet incisive account of this confluence. They were presented by Joseph Margolis on June 9th, 10th and 11th 2016 at Ca' Foscari University in Venice. The brainchild of Luigi Perissinotto, the Venice Lectures have become a prestigious tradition at Ca' Foscari: I am deeply honored to have had the opportunity to organize them through the support of the Central European Pragmatist Forum and the valuable help of the Society for the Advancement of American Philosophy.

This introduction will at first try to briefly sketch some of the crucial thematic aspects of Margolis' thought, in order to then focus on the main thesis suggested by the *Lectures* themselves.

It is not easy to distinguish one topic from another — aesthetic issues from epistemological ones or anthropological questions from ontological ones — because the mutual implications are frequent and a fruitful

---

3   Roberto Gronda, *La persistenza della tradizione: Bernstein, McDermott, Margolis e Rescher*, in Rosa Calcaterra, Giovanni Maddalena, Giancarlo Marchetti, *Il pragmatismo. Dalle origini agli sviluppi contemporanei* (Rome: Carocci, 2015), pp. 265–285.

circularity is overtly assumed. However, to ensure a certain clarity in my exposition, I will try to focus on a series of relatively distinct topics.

Finally, it is worth noting something that is apparently missing from this introduction. Margolis' readers are used to hearing him vividly distinguish his own discourse by contrast to other positions in the current debate. His sharp and frequently ironic dialectic is a constitutive part of his philosophical and literary style. However, having to write an introductory essay on Joseph Margolis' philosophy, I have preferred to focus the readers' attention directly on his own positions with regard to some central philosophical issues. But there is also another reason why I have chosen to present the mediated as unmediated (to resort to a formula *à la* Hegel): as this text is just an introduction, it is only meant to foreshadow the actual reading of Margolis' *Lectures*, which will restore the original richness of both his style and thought.

1. *On the definition of art and why it matters even outside aesthetics*

> Yes, I think that my work has really come out from my notion of aesthetics. First of all, you can't do any pertinent work in the philosophy of art, history, or culture without admitting relativism. You cannot have a theory of interpretation regarding art or the rest of the cultural world of humans that does not accommodate the relativistic option.[4]

In Italy Joseph Margolis is known above all for his work in the aesthetic field: his name usually appears together with those of the analytic philosophers who took part in the debate on the definition of art and his essays are mentioned in the various collected volumes that have introduced analytic aesthetics into our country over the last fifteen years.

However, his work on aesthetics is far from being a kind of over-specialized inquiry, basically separated and independent from other crucial philosophical issues. Even if he has always been sensitive to the technical details of the subject, Margolis has claimed that a definition of what a work of art is cannot be pursued without being aware of its basic connections with the rest of our cultural world and with a conception of what it is to be a human self. In other words, even the first superficial impression of over-technicality that is sometimes made by earlier formulations of his theory cannot be understood without referring to the wider backdrop of

---

4   Joseph Margolis, 'Interview with Joseph Margolis', p. 314.

a philosophy of culture and of an anthropology of the peculiar cultural entities we humans are.

Nonetheless, Margolis does not refuse to face the typical analytic challenge of defining art. His point is rather a double one — which actually raises many difficulties for the traditional analytic approach to the definition of art. On the one hand, he problematizes the almost obvious assumption that we cannot have a definition of art if we cannot have a generalized concept of art. This idea derives from the assumption that a definition cannot but be "exhaustive of all art and exclusive of all that is not art"[5] — that is, it is connected to a metaphysics of permanence and of an underlying unchanging order of being.[6] If we reject this kind of metaphysical framework we can discover and accept many different historical conceptions of what a work of art is, definitions which are more or less informal, more or less extensive and always connected to the relatively precarious rules of a historical form of life.

On the other hand Margolis definitely provides a definition of art that does not exclusively apply to artistic products: on the contrary, it can be extended to most of our cultural world, including us humans. From this point of view, his definition of works of art as "physically embodied and culturally emergent entities"[7] can be considered analogous to Dewey's claim that in order to understand what art is we have to return to the basic features characterizing human beings' experience of their own environment. In other words, Margolis' definition of works of art cannot be used to strictly distinguish them in comparison to other kinds of cultural or artifactual things. I have no space here to develop this point, but it is enough to say that Margolis' goal in defining art and the fruitfulness of his strategy amount to a broader move in a new and different direction: they constitute an attempt to understand the peculiarly human condition and the distinctively human word.

In any case, Margolis' famous idea of "works of art as physically embodied and culturally emergent entities" is essentially based on embodiment and emergence. The first category helped Margolis answer analytic requests for a relatively precise extensional identification of the work of art. Works of art are real things, things no less real than physical

---

5   Joseph Margolis, 'The Importance of Being Earnest about the Definition and Metaphysics of Art', *The Journal of Aesthetics and Art Criticism*, 3/68 (2010), p. 6.

6   Cf. Joseph Margolis, *The Arts and the Definition of the Human. Toward a Philosophical Anthropology*, Standford: Stanford University Press, 2009.

7   Joseph Margolis, 'Works of Art as Physically Embodied and Culturally Emergent Entities', *The British Journal of Aesthetics*, 3/14 (1974), pp. 187–196.

entities: they help construct our world and they can cause deep changes in it, even if causal efficiency is not the most suitable means by which to interpret cultural dynamics. The second category meets the need to account for the peculiarities of the cultural world, which Margolis characterizes in terms of "Intentionality". By Intentional properties Margolis means the expressive, symbolic, meaningful, semiotic, and linguistic features characterizing our cultural world. He overtly rejects Brentano's and Husserl's basically solipsistic, non-cultural and a-historical perspectives on intentionality — this is the reason why he adopts a capital 'I'. Moreover, his remark about the Intentional characteristics of the human world has nothing to do with a mere subjective or private characterization of the world itself, nor with a primarily mental treatment of our experience. On the contrary, for Margolis Intentionality is strictly connected to the social character of human conditions: by Intentional properties he means those attributes we can ascribe to something or someone because they are already embedded within a shared world of practices; those practices are essentially connected to the fact that from birth we have to learn a natural language from a social group and to acquire the informal rules governing a certain common form of life. Such properties emerge from mere physical properties and cannot be reduced to them, even though they cannot exist apart from the real world we live in. This is the reason why Margolis speaks of "artifactual transformation" — of producing works of art — as a kind of ontological transformation or metaphysical construction, which nonetheless maintains a deeply realistic claim.

Emergence, however, has been shown to have broader implications over the last few years, when the analogy between the emergence of works of art from physical media and the emergence of self-conscious creatures from human animals has been overtly developed. Whereas in the 1970s Margolis' aim was to ensure a materialistic or realistic treatment of art while avoiding any form of reduction of cultural entities to mere physical things, in the 1990s and in the first decade of the 21st century his basic insight is that we cannot properly deal with cultural artifacts if we do not address the problem of the cultural peculiarities of the human world against the background of a basic animal continuity.[8] In other words, "you cannot formulate a reasonable theory of the arts — the fine arts — without providing a pertinent sketch of the relationship between nature and

---

8   See Joseph Margolis, *The Arts and the Definition of the Human*, and Joseph
     Margolis, 'Placing Artworks — Placing Ourselves', *Journal of Chinese
     Philosophy*, 1/31 (2004), pp. 1–16.

culture".[9] There is nothing extravagant or vainly rhetorical in comparing persons and works of art: on the contrary, Margolis is focusing on what he characterizes as the "artifactuality of persons", that is the constructive dimension of being humans in relation to their physiological or biological nature. From his perspective, to be a person is to be a second-natured entity: the human organism transforms itself into a person or into a self by acquiring a natural language and the connected socially shared practices — both verbal competencies and lingual or significant ones. The point of arrival will be a deep reinforcement of Margolis' thesis that we are beings characterized by an enlanguaged form of life. Becoming humans is conceived as a historical process, open to the actions of the cultural and social world we share with others, and it is conceived as a process where we are constantly constructing and reconstructing our own self-identities in relation to others.[10]

2. *Earnest relativism*

> [...] relativism is a conceptually respectable option that fits our
> intuitions rather neatly in a variety of contexts without giving way
> to incoherence or mere arbitrariness.[11]

As the quotation introducing the previous section suggests, from the very beginning it was Margolis' inquiry into the peculiarities of aesthetic judgments that pushed him towards the formulation of a kind of robust relativism, capable of assuming a more complex set of values than the one involved in the traditional binary logic of true and false — dependent upon the exclusion of the third middle.

In other words, it is the complexity of our cultural world that leads Margolis to affirm the need for a form of relativism as a kind of approach that is better tailored to cultural artifacts and is even required by their peculiar Intentional, contingent, and historical properties.

In Margolis' pivotal essay *Robust Relativism* the point of departure is the typically aesthetic issue of the validity claims of aesthetic judgments,

---

9   Joseph Margolis, *The Deviant Ontology of Artworks*, in Noel Carroll (ed.), *Theories of Art Today*, (Madison-London: The University of Wisconsin Press, 2000), p. 117.
10   See Joseph Margolis, *Towards a Metaphysics of Culture*.
11   Joseph Margolis, 'The Reasonableness of Relativism', *Philosophy and Phenomenological Research*, 1/43 (1982), pp. 91–92.

traditionally understood as the pretension to be true and not false. The trouble is that, when judging artistic products, very often we are faced with overtly incongruent judgments — judgments that would be mutually incompatible within a bivalent logic admitting only true or false values, even if there are good reasons to sustain every incongruent judgment. But why should we reject judgments that are based on pertinent arguments and justifying reasons to support them? The way out for Margolis consists in the explicit assumption of a wider set of values than that involved in a binary logic: while some judgments are clearly false, because no rigorous argumentation is or even could be provided to support them, other judgments, which show some cogency, must be assumed to be as reasonable, admissible, understandable, plausible or apt. There are many "third" possibilities that fall between "true" and "false" or between "right" and "wrong". The point made in the 1976 essay is that if we acknowledge that works of art are emergent cultural entities, we must be able to deal with their distinctive feature, namely their being open to alternative descriptions and being subject to the "proliferation of intensional divergences".[12] This means that the art world and the cultural world more generally require a "relativistic account of value", which leaves room for other kinds of logic compatible with a relativistic logic.

Over the following years, Margolis reinforced his discourse on the metaphysical implications of a bivalent logic and explicitly extended his relativistic claims to the whole human world, including the so-called natural or positive sciences.

Margolis' idea that Protagoras' position was oversimplified and misunderstood by both Plato and Aristotle is complementary to his thesis that our belief in the compelling nature of the logic of true and false is connected to a metaphysics of immutability according to which everything real must possess an unchanging structure precisely in order be real.[13] But this equation between real and fixed is far from obvious. On the contrary, from the radically contingent, historical perspective openly adopted by Margolis, he cannot but dispute the legitimacy of the concept of immutability and even of its modern version according to which nature is governed by unchanging, universal laws, admitting no exceptions.[14] If

---

12   Joseph Margolis, *Robust Relativism*, p. 44.
13   See Ugo Zilioli, 'Un relativismo robusto. Genealogia e forza di un'idea', *Discipline filosofiche* 2007/2(2007), pp. 51–70.
14   See Joseph Margolis, *What, After All, Is a Work of Art: Lectures in the Philosophy of Art*, (University Park: The Pennsylvania State University Press, 1999), p. 41 and ff. and Joseph Margolis, *The Arts and the Definition of the Human*, the *Prologue*.

we reject this metaphysical framework, a multivalued logic appears to be just as coherent as a binary logic, based on the principle of the excluded middle.

Marginalizing the Intentional properties of the cultural world because they poorly conform to a false/true logic would mean denying the reality of the cultural world itself. In other terms, from Margolis' point of view, this kind of theoretical move would imply denying human existence *tout court*, because human beings themselves are culturally constituted, they are *homines sapientes* who turn into persons or selves by acquiring a mother language, by becoming used to the informal regularities ruling a certain collective group and by becoming competent members of a situated, shared form of life. From this point of view, relativism is compatible with the kind of realistic constructivism adopted by Margolis, but is also viable and responsible with respect to the peculiarities of the human condition. In other words, "In this sense, relativism is a reminder of our epistemic frailties".[15]

As already mentioned, Margolis' further step is to extend the relativistic claim outside the arts and the so-called human sciences. If we accept the thesis of the artifactuality of persons, everything we contribute to construct — the facts of nature we investigate in physics and chemistry or the life processes we study in biology — belongs to the cultural world. The ultimate consequence of this is the constructivist form of realism supported by Joseph Margolis, according to which we cannot sharply distinguish the natural world from the cultural one and we must consider the possibility that a relativistic logic could be more appropriate than a bivalent logic for the symbiotic situation of encultured human animals.

It seems as though this topic is not simply a theoretical one among others; it rather appears to be the answer to the almost moral obligation to explicitly consider the ultimate consequences of the philosophical path we choose to develop: if we adopt a radically contingent view of our world and if we recognize both the animal continuity characterizing us as humans and the cultural peculiarities distinguishing us because of our lack of a specific environmental place in the world, we have to accept relativism — a rigorous relativism, based on pertinent arguments and justified reasons — as our best chance. In my view, Margolis partly adopts this position in contrast to the other great figures of neo-pragmatism, who refused in various way to consider relativism a serious option.[16]

---

15   Joseph Margolis, *What, After All, Is a Work of Art*, p. 64.
16   See David Hildebrand, *Margolis's Pragmatism of Continuity*, in Dirk-Martin Grube, Robert Sinclair (ed.), *Pragmatism, Metaphysics and Culture. Reflextions*

3. *Realistic constructivism and radical historicism*

> There is no first principle of reality or knowledge or reason that
> must be settled before all other philosophical questions may be
> effectively answered. Certainly, there is no widespread agreement
> about what determinate form such a principle should take.
> There is also little prospect of agreeing on any first principle
> unless the real world has a discernibly changeless order.
> But if it had such a structure, then, in an obvious sense, that
> would provide the decisive first principle on which diverging
> philosophical policies could jointly claim to rely.
> Hence, short of establishing the facts of invariance — which
> innumerable philosophies have pursued in bewilderingly different
> ways — it would be a best counterstrategy to demonstrate why such
> a principle would be unlikely or impossible to confirm.[17]

The last point touched upon in the previous section brings us to the
core of Margolis' metaphysical assumption. To his disenchanted eyes,
it must be acknowledged that the natural world is objectively there as
something independent from us and that we can distinguish it from our
cultural constructions: this is the realistic or materialistic side of Margolis'
claim. He always asserts the reality of the cultural world against the
typical analytic move of considering all those properties and events
characterized by Intentionality and their qualitative or informal statute as
unreal or at least as marginal and liable to reduction. However, we also
have to acknowledge that we can make this kind of distinction only from
within: facts — even natural facts — are not what could be identified
independently from any inquiry, but what is posited as independent with
reference to a certain inquiry or within an inquiry.[18] This is a thesis about
the form of objectivity we can reasonably support from within the space
of the human enlanguaged experience of the world — a position which is
explicitly indebted to Hegel's response to Kant and that has something to
share with Margolis' interpretation of Dewey's *Logic*, as the third *Venetian
Lecture* illustrates. Kuhn and Wittgenstein's *Philosophical Investigations*

---

on the Philosophy of Joseph Margolis (Helsinki: Nordic Pragmatism Network, 2015), pp. 37–51.

17   Joseph Margolis, *Historied Thought, Constructed World. A Conceptual Primer for the Turn of the Millenium*, (Berkeley, Los Angeles, Oxford: University of California Press, 1995), p. 23.

18   Joseph Margolis, 'Objectivity as a Problem: An Attempt at an Overview', *The Annals of the American Academy of Political and Social Science*, 560 (1998), pp. 55–68.

are also crucial elements flowing into this stream: "there is no neutral place from which to look at propositions first and then at facts and then check to see whether indeed they matched one another".[19] Moreover, there is no privileged third ground from which we can disentangle this kind of issue once and for all. The point is that, because of its being culturally emergent from naturalistic dispositions and features, the human framework is characterized by a sort of indissoluble symbiosis between the world we live in and the shared language and practices we develop from within.[20] Hence, *"there is no formal procedure for fixing reference uniquely, regardless of one's theory of real particulars, real entities, real referents"*.[21] However in ordinary life this is not a problem for the most part, because *"reference succeeds in a practical way without requiring any such rigor"*;[22] and of course one may ask why this kind of tolerance is typical and maybe even required by the human form of life. But I do not wish to jump here to the anthropological implications entailed by Margolis' position, which will be dealt with later on.

Here it might be best to connect Margolis' realistic constructivism with his ideas about the constructed nature of the human historied world, which has been articulated in detail in his *Historied Thought, Constructed World*.[23]

History essentially characterizes both the human condition and the human world: it is a human construction whereby humans constitute themselves and the cultural world, including the scientific world. This does not mean that we have to embrace an idealistic perspective, Margolis argues, as though history and the world were mere subjective productions. For sure, we meet the resistance of a 'brute' world, but this circumstance only occurs from within the distinctively symbiotic human condition, intertwining with nature and culture. Hence, the main element characterizing a "theory of radical history" is that "we have no reason to think the real world is invariantly structured, distributively structured in any fixedly essential or necessary way".[24]

---

19   Joseph Margolis, 'Objectivity as a Problem: An Attempt at an Overview', p. 60.
20   Phillip Honenberger, *The Poverty of Neo-Pragmatism: Rorty, Putnam and Margolis on Realism and Relativism*, in Dirk-Martin Grube, Robert Sinclair (ed.), *Pragmatism, Metaphysics and Culture. Reflextions on the Philosophy of Joseph Margolis* (Helsinki: Nordic Pragmatism Network, 2015), pp. 76–99.
21   Joseph Margolis, 'Prospects for a Theory of Radical History', in *The Monist*, 1/74 (1991), p. 282.
22   Joseph Margolis, 'Prospects for a Theory of Radical History', p. 282.
23   Joseph Margolis, *Historied Thought, Constructed World*.
24   Joseph Margolis, 'Prospects for a Theory of Radical History', p. 283.

Margolis' reason for abandoning the metaphysical pretension to fixity is very clear: a changing or historied world is much more plausible from a standpoint that refers not only to human contributions from within — by looking at material and practical changes — but also to cultural, artistic and even scientific contributions. What is radically new in his theory of history is the idea that it is not conceptually necessary for reality to possess an invariant nature or structure. It would be conceptually necessary only if knowledge and inquiry could discern an independent invariant order. But the point Margolis always emphazises is that the different orders we know and practice are structurally "dependent on the contingent symbiosis of knower and known".[25] There is no way out of this symbiosis, because it constitutes the way in which we humans are and belong to the real world.

4. *Pragmatism as naturalism without reductions*

> Still, one is likely to protest: 'But pragmatism is already a
> naturalism'. Of course it is, but not of the 'right sort'![26]

Over the last decades this American philosopher has also come to be known in Italy as a pragmatist: Margolis' books and essays are known within the rather narrow circle of those with an interest in pragmatism, thanks to the work of Rosa Calcaterra and the Pragma Association. His rather late espousing of the pragmatist cause is extremely significant for understanding his thought, even though it is obvious that pragmatism is far from being his only philosophical wellspring.[27]

After his exposure to the last voices of classical pragmatism during his early years as a university student,[28] Joseph Margolis abandoned this philosophical approach for other perspectives, for analytic philosophy in the 1950s and 1960s, while inquiring into phenomenology and classic German

25 Joseph Margolis, 'Prospects for a Theory of Radical History', p. 283.
26 Joseph Margolis, *Reinventing Pragmatism. American Philosophy at the End of the Twentieth Century*, Ithaca and London: Cornell University Press, 2002, p. 5.
27 Wittgenstein's *Philosophical Investigations* (Wittgenstein 2009) together with Kuhn's *Structure of Scientific Revolutions* (Kuhn 1970) and Hegel's *Phenomenology of the Spirit* (Hegel 1977) (a polished version of Hegel, without what Margolis calls his philosophical "extravagances"), could be identified -, I would suggest — as his chief points of reference. To these influences we have to add those of the post-Darwinian scientist and philosophers, Adolf Portmann and Marjorie Grene.
28 Joseph Margolis, 'Interview with Joseph Margolis'.

philosophy in the 1970s. However, starting in the 1980s, pragmatism awoke in him the idea of a third and more feasible alternative to the limits of both the above-mentioned philosophical approaches — limits that were coming to the surface from both within and without the analytical and the continental traditions. As he states in *Pragmatism's Advantage*, he found in classical pragmatism a viable alternative, on the one hand, to the kind of scientific reductionism which was becoming dominant in analytic philosophy in the form of the so-called naturalizing of philosophy, and, on the other hand, to the continental tendency to escape "the life and capacities of ordinary human beings",[29] by adopting a general transcendental stance.

At the same time, classical pragmatism showed a capacity to combine its realistic or materialistic stance with the crucial Kantian-Hegelian heritage, that is with the basic idea that "there cannot be a disjunction between the human subject and its world".[30] This last issue can be seen as the point of departure of the particular kind of realistic constructivism developed by Joseph Margolis — the ultimate consequence of which is represented by his explicit commitment to robust relativism. The previous sections of this introduction have already considered these features of Margolis' mature thought.

However, with reference to the above-mentioned characteristics, we could say that in pragmatism Margolis found two further opportunities. The first was the possibility to develop a form of naturalism that is not reductive — to elaborate a natural but not naturalized approach to philosophical issues. The second opportunity was to develop a theory about the hybrid being of human persons, by taking into account both the basic natural continuity between man and the other animals and the distinctive features characterizing humans as self-reflexive creatures or as culturally constructed selves. Dewey's cultural naturalism and his deep anti-dualism are therefore the most attractive resources found in pragmatism according to Margolis, resources that must nonetheless be clarified and further developed according to him.

The first point involves a sharp distinction between the form of naturalism characterizing the classical pragmatists and the current trend towards the naturalization of philosophical problems, according to which they should be turned into scientific issues or at any rate dealt with as such — a theoretical move which is now generally associated with Quine's pivotal

---

29   Joseph Margolis, 'Pragmatism's Advantage', *History of Philosophy Quaterly*, 2/21 (2004), p. 208.
30   Joseph Margolis, 'Pragmatism's Advantage', p. 204.

essay *Epistemology Naturalized.*[31] This distinction is also crucial according to Margolis because in the neopragmatist debate a pragmatist option for naturalism is often blended with the kind of scientism or physicalism that can be considered the legacy of a certain strand of analytic philosophy.

In his *Prologue* to *Reinventing Pragmatism* Margolis sums up the crucial aspects characterizing the current naturalizing trend. According to this perspective, the only explanations which can be considered truth-bearing are causal ones — and causality is essentially restricted to linear, efficient causality. Moreover, the main assumption is that causal explanations must be committed to the so-called "causal closure of the physical" — where it is evident that physical entities are assumed as the paradigmatic (if not exclusive) specimens of reality and are supposed to have been caused by other physical processes. These conditions lead to two basic consequences: the first is supervenience, apparently the only (problematic) alternative to eliminativism when dealing with mental or cultural phenomena; the second consequence is that every explanation that does not conform to the above-mentioned conditions is considered to be "philosophically illegitimate".[32]

This picture makes it quite clear that not only is the naturalism of the classic pragmatists one of a different sort, but that from Margolis' perspective it also provides a more adequate tool for considering the human world. First of all, naturalism had the basic — but not futile — meaning of refusing "to admit non-natural or supernatural resources in the descriptive or explanatory discourse of any truth-bearing kind":[33] this is a very promising feature of pragmatism for Margolis, because it explicitly rejects any form of transcendentalism or essentialism that seeks, in either Continentalist or Analytic ways, to escape the radically contingent world we belong to. The very title of the second chapter of Dewey's 1925 *Experience and Nature*, *Existence as precarious and as stable,*[34] is eloquent from this perspective. On the other hand, the kind of "*cultural* naturalism" overtly adopted by Dewey's *Logic. The Theory of Inquiry*[35] is understood as an attempt to deal with the distinctive features of culture in the human world against the

---

31   Willard Van Orman Quine, *Epistemology Naturalized*, in *Ontological Relativity and Other Essays*, (New York: Columbia University Press, 1969), pp. 69–90.

32   Joseph Margolis, *Reinventing Pragmatism*, p. 7.

33   Joseph Margolis, *Reinventing Pragmatism*, p. 6.

34   John Dewey, *Experience and Nature*, in *The Later Works, 1925-1953, Volume 1* (Carbondale and Edwardsville: Southern Illinois University Press, 1988).

35   John Dewey, *Logic. The Theory of Inquiry*, in *The Later Works, 1925-1953, Volume 12* (Carbondale and Edwardsville: Southern Illinois University Press, 1991).

background of what we could describe as an emergentist picture: while cultural phenomena arise from the very conditions of our natural world, including the biological or physiological conditions of the human form of life, the new kinds of cultural configurations that emerge cannot be reduced to their physical bases. Intentional entities, properties and events contribute to modifying the contingent and open structure of our world. Hence here Margolis can find confirmation of his claim that not only physical entities are real and that cultural phenomena need not be subject to the categories of the mere (or allegedly mere) physical world. The peculiarities of the cultural world must be seriously considered by rejecting both any form of physical reductionism or eliminativism and any recourse to extra-naturalistic sources as a means to explain its emergence. At the same time, causality appears to take place in a variety of forms, which cannot be oversimplified by taking efficient causation as the standard model.

The second opportunity, which the theorist of the hybrid nature of man finds in classical pragmatism, has again Dewey's *Experience and Nature* at its basis. Here we can find a serious attempt to consider human beings within a "generously Darwinized ecology"[36] as "the non-cognitive animal condition" of human epistemology.[37] Actual human beings take the place of the transcendental ego: cultured animals with their habits, emotions, and enlanguaged experience take the place of the allegedly disembodied solipsistic consciousness of transcendental philosophy.

Moreover, the classical pragmatism of Dewey — and Mead, I would add — offers an alternative way to consider the self-reflective character of persons as distinct from primates. Dewey, Margolis says, never sought to eliminate all references to the mental dimension in dealing with human animals. On the contrary, the goal he was pursuing was to reject any account of the psychic or mental as something radically private — as something whose determination does not depend on human interactions with a natural and naturally social environment but, on the contrary, is presupposed by these interactions.[38] We can and indeed must speak about intimate thoughts, individual feelings and even mental images. But the crucial point is that they cannot be supposed to lay at the origin of our experience as the primitive features essentially composing it. On the contrary, they derive from the social and broadly enlanguaged experience of the world we share with other people from birth.

---

36   Joseph Margolis, 'Pragmatism's Advantage', p. 207.
37   Joseph Margolis, *Reinventing Pragmatism*, p. 110.
38   Joseph Margolis, 'Pragmatism's Advantage', p. 217.

5. *The* Venetian Lectures

The *Venetian Lectures* are ideally intended to outline a kind of philosophical anthropology that weaves together the various strands of Margolis' thought, as already noted at the beginning of this paper. The development and acquisition of natural languages play a crucial role in Margolis' picture of the hybrid history of humanity.

The central issue is the problem of the human "gap" in animal continuity: this is the basic paradox characterizing human beings and Margolis' challenge is to interpret the distinctiveness of man — Intentional and cultural phenomena in the above-explained sense and the self-reflexive character of human persons — without recurring to extra-naturalized causes or sources, and while avoiding any form of eliminativism or reduction of the personal and the cultural to physical entities. If we give up the ancient idea that man is an exception in nature because of his allegedly divine origin, this does not mean that we have to adopt a reductivist approach, by eliminating the cultural and self-reflexive peculiarities naturally characterizing the human world. The point, on the contrary, is that Margolis is ready to acknowledge the complexity of the animal world — both in its social aspects and in its non-discursive forms of rationality.

Margolis' critical point of departure is the problematization of a thesis supported by some of the most outstanding post-Darwinian scholars of today: being social is an extremely important feature of being human, but it is not enough to understand the emergence of human persons, because this means overlooking the highly refined forms of societal life characterizing many animal species — where nonetheless we cannot appreciate the level of self-reflexivity that is distinctive of human beings. On the contrary, acquiring a natural language remains a distinctively human characteristic: although it is grounded in the completely natural favorable changes in the human vocal apparatus and brain, it contributes to producing the processual construction of selves out of human animals. Margolis does not hesitate here to speak of a metaphysical transformation of human primates into selves or persons, exactly as he did when supporting the idea that works of art emerge as new kinds of entities from other kinds of things or properties — whose reality cannot be denied by viewing physical entities as the sole or paradigmatic kind of real entity. Although this kind of vocabulary can engender some misunderstanding, Margolis is not considering language as a transcendental condition of possibility of humanity. He is thinking about effective, spoken languages, which are found in distinctively human and always contingent contexts. The genesis of language among human primates is understood as a wholly natural and casual process, which nonetheless produces effective changes in the previous configuration of the natural world.

Moreover, we cannot speak about a kind of causal link between language acquisition by early hominids and by human infants and their becoming self-reflexive persons with narrative identities. On the contrary, the two changes are understood as the two faces of the same process. In other words, humans produce natural languages that, while founded on the peculiarities of human physiology, develop as a means to configure meanings that overtly exceed the mere physiological action of noises or sounds. The hybrid character of natural language, in turn, contributes to shaping humans as self-reflective beings, whose ways of operating within the environment are always naturally charged with meaning in the widest sense of the term. In other words, the history of the genesis of languages and of humans is a circular one and we have no privileged external vantage point from which to examine it: the contingent emergence of natural languages introduces something new in the world of early hominids, something which reacts on them by transforming them into human persons. But only human selves can speak to one another — no mere hominid can do so. There is no single solution to the problem, but Margolis accepts the aporetical aspect of the question. There is no means to grasp an allegedly independent truth about the very nature of things, given that warranted assertability is the only second-best chance we can count on within a radically contingent perspective and this is one of the cases where we must agree recognize with the pragmatist that life is already there before our cognitively oriented questions are posed.

Paraphrasing John Dewey, we could state that understanding human experience as a paradigmatically or eminently cognitive enterprise is one of the illusory fallacies of traditional philosophy that must definitely be rejected.

This issue is one of the final focuses of the third *Lecture*, but in the first two lectures, in my opinion, the so-called "mongrel functionality" of ordinary language represents a new key element. In the background, an overt engagement takes place with the various voices of what Margolis considers a potentially regressive rationalistic trend in present neo-pragmatism. This has to do with the ideal of analytic clarity applied to language, which led not only Frege and Russell, but also, according to Margolis, the late Wittgenstein to understand philosophy as a battle against the enchantments of language. On the contrary, Margolis urges us to focus on the fact that human languages very often work in a mongrel and informal way, tolerating a certain degree of vagueness and even mistakes. In other words, we must take into account the fact that we cannot completely transform all opacity and vagueness into clarity. Nonetheless, he invites the reader to consider this relative indeterminacy of language not as a kind of defective situation in need to be corrected or contained, but as a structural element characterizing our enlanguaged experience of the world, and playing a basically positive role in human experience. To sum all this up in a formula, Margolis provides an image of *le langage de l'à peu près* working under or together with *le langage de la precision* — the latter in turn representing a relatively small portion of our effectively spoken languages.

Rather than being a defective exception in need of correction, according to Joseph Margolis, the mongrel functionality of ordinary language is definitely a resource for human animals both from an evolutionary perspective and with reference to the functioning of everyday verbal interchanges. First of all, the mongrel, informal, approximate, imprecise and relatively indeterminate functioning of mutual understanding and converging on a common reference appears to be as a crucial feature for a form of living that is connected neither to a specific environmental niche nor to a precisely prefigured *telos*. It lends flexibility, plasticity and swifter adaptability to different contexts and a more agile convergence on common goals to our moving in the world around us. By shifting the focus onto ordinary interchanges, mongrel language is good enough to face everyday circumstances, to discount many problems which should arise if we had to deal with every circumstance in our life with the highest degree of accuracy and precision. It provides us with our sense of the real world, which is partly made up of vagueness, inaccuracy and striking yet ultimately acceptable errors (as in the case of the assumed dualism between body and mind), but is good enough to live with; and it allows us to focus more attentively on other issues. Only prolonged immersion in a shared language and culture enables us to reach deeply informal, but consequently stable and silently consensual references. This is true (in the mongrel sense of the word "true"!) for ordinary language as much as for most of our specialized philosophical language: Margolis invites us to acknowledge that what is relevant for supporting a specific theoretical assumption is more the plausibility of its use than some algorithm-like cogency — as is the case with most of our beliefs about the nature of the world, our own mind, or that of others.

A further important contribution of Margolis' *Venetian Lectures* is constituted by his focus on the collective dimension of human forms of life. Margolis already emphasized the distinction between collective terms and aggregated ones in the past (Margolis 1986): a linguistic exchange can only take place within a shared linguistic space, which cannot be considered the aggregate sum of individual linguistic acts, because it must already be there in order for an individual linguistic utterance to happen. From this perspective, Margolis has criticized any mentalistic and solipsistic strategy in philosophy as being essentially unable to draw this kind of distinction.

I would argue that from Margolis' pragmatist perspective the sharing of an enlanguaged experience with other people from birth is something not susceptible to mistrust, by way of a Cartesian form of doubt: our existence is largely verbal and likewise lingual, that is significant in connection to common practices and forms of life that are partaken by human selves or persons, whose narrative identities emerge only within the enlanguaged experience they share.

Hence, in the third *Lecture* Margolis suggests a reinterpretation of Wittgenstein's concept of *Lebensform*: this is not only the collective, shared mode of living we have in common and we are dynamically configuring and re-configuring from within. Rather, it should be understood as the whole process of internal and external constitution of the human self, whose shaping takes place in a common space, via mutual reactions and interactions. If the personal pronoun "I" is almost nothing at the beginning of its history, it acquires depth and substance through the interchanges with others within a shared linguistic space and a common form of life. It gradually becomes a real person by acquiring a narrative, whose components are a multitude of different voices. It is a mongrel, hybrid process, but nonetheless an effective one.

The last *Venetian Lecture* was originally delivered by Joseph Margolis as his contribution as keynote speaker to the Central European Pragmatist Forum Conference. Nonetheless, it definitely seems to draw its conclusions about the status of human norms from the theoretical framework outlined in the previous lectures. Margolis' engagement with the different positions adopted by John Rawls (and Habermas) on the allegedly universal character of norms is closely connected not only to his opting for radical historicism, but also to his considerations on the modes of being characterizing human forms of life in comparison to other living organisms.

If we adopt a radically historical view of the human world, we must abandon the idea that an absolute foundation of moral theory is possible. Kant's search of a-historical norms valid for the whole of humanity is a noble quest, but it must be dropped, given the historical contingency of human societies, whose configurations continually change in unexpected ways. All too often the claim of having discovered universal norms that should be applied to the whole of humanity proves merely an extension of a "customary morality" — to evoke the formula Dewey used in his *Ethics* (Dewey 1985) — to other people, whose *èthos* had been developing in different ways.

Of course, this is a dangerous enterprise, but Margolis sees no other way out of the radical contingency of the human condition. If we adopt a post-Darwinian conception of humans as linguistic beings, casually emerging through cultural-biological evolution, and hence as intrinsically hybrid, artifactual and historical beings, without a predestined niche in the world nor a fixed natural or rational *telos* to realize, we cannot make a claim to universal or necessary norms, supposed to regulate every form of human life. However, Margolis' point is that we still have regularities, *sittliche* norms and rules, ranging from more informal, habitual — but in many cases no less compelling — rules of behavior to more explicit, rationalized and formalized norms. In other terms, principles and norms appear to be rooted in largely mongrel, informal and approximate practices, demonstrating that, even if we acknowledge that our norms are artifactual, this does not at all mean that we can construe the norms we want. On the contrary, our explicit norms respond to a certain *èthos* that is already there and hinges on our common modes of behavior, in the shared space of a *Lebensform* already there before we can reflexively develop our morals.

Even in relation to this last point, Margolis seems to converge with a crucial aspect of Dewey's pragmatism: reflexive morality, together with inquiring reason, is one of the best resources on which we can and must rely, but we cannot forget that it is a secondary move, that it does not come as the first step.

To conclude, in this last lecture Joseph Margolis is pushing us to acknowledge and further develop the diverse implications and consequences involved in our being humans — without foregoing his unique style, consisting in a peculiar combination of irony and philosophical honesty.[39]

---

39 I am very grateful to Tom Rockmore, David Hildebrand and Joseph Margolis for some precious comments on this paper.

A shorter version of the First Lecture has been published in *Pragmatism Today*, 7, 2, 2016, pp. 8–22. A French translation of the Second Lecture is forthcoming in *Archives de Philosophie*.

Bibliography

Dewey J., *Ethics*, in *The Later Works, 1925-1953, Volume 7* (Carbondale and Edwardsville: Southern Illinois University Press, 1985).

Dewey J., *Experience and Nature*, in *The Later Works, 1925-1953, Volume 1* (Carbondale and Edwardsville: Southern Illinois University Press, 1988).

Dewey J., *Logic. The Theory of Inquiry*, in *The Later Works, 1925-1953, Volume 12* (Carbondale and Edwardsville: Southern Illinois University Press, 1991).

Gronda R., *La persistenza della tradizione: Bernstein, McDermott, Margolis e Rescher*, in Rosa Calcaterra, Giovanni Maddalena, Giancarlo Marchetti, *Il pragmatismo. Dalle origini agli sviluppi contemporanei* (Rome: Carocci, 2015), pp. 265–285.

Grube D.M., Sinclair R. (ed.), *Pragmatism, Metaphysics and Culture. Reflextions on the Philosophy of Joseph Margolis* (Helsinki: Nordic Pragmatism Network, 2015).

Hegel G.W.F., *Phenomenology of Spirit*, (Oxford: Oxford University Press, 1977).

Hildebrand D., *Margolis's Pragmatism of Continuity*, in Dirk-Martin Grube, Robert Sinclair (ed.), *Pragmatism, Metaphysics and Culture. Reflextions on the Philosophy of Joseph Margolis* (Helsinki: Nordic Pragmatism Network, 2015), pp. 37–51.

Honenberger P., *The Poverty of Neo-Pragmatism: Rorty, Putnam and Margolis on Realism and Relativism*, in Dirk-Martin Grube, Robert Sinclair (ed.), *Pragmatism, Metaphysics and Culture. Reflextions on the Philosophy of Joseph Margolis* (Helsinki: Nordic Pragmatism Network, 2015), pp. 76–99.

Kuhn T., *The Structure of Scientific Revolutions*, (Chicago: University of Chicago Press, 1970).

Margolis J., 'Works of Art as Physically Embodied and Culturally Emergent Entities', *The British Journal of Aesthetics*, 3/14 (1974), pp. 187–196.

Margolis J., 'Robust Relativism', *The Journal of Aesthetics and Art Criticism*, 1/35 (1976), pp. 37–46.

Margolis J., 'Persons: Notes on their Nature, Identity, and Rationality', *Southern Journal of Philosophy*, 4/18 (1980), pp. 463–472.

Margolis J., 'The Reasonableness of Relativism', *Philosophy and Phenomenological Research*, 1/43 (1982), pp. 91–97.

Margolis J., 'Intentionality, Institutions, and Human Nature', *The Monist*, 4/69 (1986), pp. 546–567.

Margolis J., 'Prospects for a Theory of Radical History', in *The Monist*, 1/74 (1991), pp. 268–292.

Margolis J., *Historied Thought, Constructed World. A Conceptual Primer for the Turn of the Millenium*, (Berkeley, Los Angeles, Oxford: University of California Press, 1995).

Margolis J., 'Objectivity as a Problem: An Attempt at an Overview', *The Annals of the American Academy of Political and Social Science*, 560 (1998), pp. 55–68.

Margolis J., *What, After All, Is a Work of Art: Lectures in the Philosophy of Art*, (University Park: The Pennsylvania State University Press, 1999), translated into Italian by Andrea Baldini, *Ma allora, che cos'è un'opera d'arte? Lezioni di filosofia dell'arte*, (Milan-Udine: Mimesis, 2007).

Margolis J., *The Deviant Ontology of Artworks*, in Noel Carroll (ed.), *Theories of Art Today*, (Madison-London: The University of Wisconsin Press, 2000) pp. 109–129.

Margolis J., *Reinventing Pragmatism. American Philosophy at the End of the Twentieth Century*, Ithaca and London: Cornell University Press, 2002.

Margolis J., 'Placing Artworks — Placing Ourselves', *Journal of Chinese Philosophy*, 1/31 (2004), pp. 1–16.

Margolis J., 'Pragmatism's Advantage', *History of Philosophy Quaterly*, 2/21 (2004), pp. 201–222.

Margolis J., *The Arts and the Definition of the Human. Toward a Philosophical Anthropology*, Standford: Stanford University Press, 2009.

Margolis J., 'The Importance of Being Earnest about the Definition and Metaphysics of Art', *The Journal of Aesthetics and Art Criticism*, 3/68 (2010), pp. 215–223.

Margolis J., 'Interview with Joseph Margolis', *European Journal for Pragmatism and American Philosophy*, VI/1 (2014), pp. 305–317.

Margolis J., 'Preparations for a Theory of Interpretation', *Contemporary Pragmatism*, 12/1 (2015), pp. 11–37.

Margolis J., *Towards a Metaphysics of Culture*, in Dirk-Martin Grube, Robert Sinclair (ed.), *Pragmatism, Metaphysics and Culture. Reflextions* on the Philosophy of Joseph Margolis (Helsinki: Nordic Pragmatism Network, 2015), pp. 1–35.

Margolis J., 'Answering Emancipation', *Pragmatism Today*, 2/6 (2015), pp. 144–153.

Quine W.V.O., *Epistemology Naturalized*, in *Ontological Relativity and Other Essays*, (New York: Columbia University Press, 1969), pp. 69–90.

Shusterman R., Krausz M.(ed.), *Interpretation, Relativism, and the Metaphysics of Culture: Themes in the Philosophy of Joseph Margolis*, (Amherst: Humanity Books, 1991).

Wittgenstein L., *Philosophical Investigations*, trans. Gertrud Elizabeth Margaret Anscombe, Peter Michael Stephan Hacker and Joachim Schulte (Oxford: Wiley-Blackwell, 2009, fourth edition), pp. 1–181.

Zilioli U., 'Un relativismo robusto. Genealogia e forza di un'idea', *Discipline filosofiche* 2007/2(2007), pp. 51–70.

Joseph Margolis

THREE PARADOXES OF PERSONHOOD:
THE VENETIAN LECTURES
WITH THE MICHAEL ELDRIDGE LECTURE
(2016)

ACKNOWLEDGEMENTS

I heartedly thank Professor Roberta Dreon for the generous invitation, in the name of the Ca' Foscari University of Venice and the Department of Philosophy and Cultural Heritage, and with the support of the Society for the Advancement of American Philosophy, to deliver the *Lezioni veneziane di Filosofia*, in Venice, June 9, 10, and 11, 2016; further, regarding the separate invitation to give the Michael Eldridge Lecture, concurrently with the *Lezioni*, at the Ninth International Conference of the Central European Pragmatism Forum (June 5-10, 2016), convened under the extended hospitality of the University and Department, I wish also to thank Professor John Ryder, on behalf of the organizing committee of the Forum, for that second invitation. I can't remember a more agreeable professional occasion. I should also like to add a word of thanks to the splendid people of Venice.

A WORD ABOUT THE *LECTURES*

The theme of these talks, the "paradoxes of personhood," came to me almost at once, on being invited to give the *Venice Lectures* for 2016. I've been puttering for some time — not unlike the way one collects stones along the beach — among potentially attractive ways of venturing a fresh analysis of what it is to be a person. (I confess I regard that question as the single most important philosophical and practical issue that we ever pose.) I am myself, have been for many years, completely absorbed with the intuition that the human self or person is an artifactual but perfectly natural transform of the primate species, *Homo sapiens sapiens*, spontaneously yielded in the uniquely completed evolution of its infant members. (I say, "uniquely," because its generative process proceeds by way of the conjoint functioning of biologically incarnated and enculturing causes, which, thus intertwined, issues finally in the appearance of the hybrid being we call "self" or "person." Effectively, human evolution profoundly challenges — very possibly defeats — the claims to adequacy of Darwin's and canonical neo-Darwinian theories of evolution. (The very meaning of "evolution" — in Darwin's argument — has been permanently and profoundly affected by the human case.)

There appear to be no comparable variants of animal evolution (among other species) effected by anything like the culturally enabled creation, *Bildung*, mastery, and transmission of true language. Of course, the human paradigm, culminating in the novel competences of persons, signals that future forms of evolution are likely to involve the intertwining of natural and technologically engineered changes affecting any and all of the contributing sub-processes of standard evolutionary theory: most notably, breeding and mutation. Continually new technologies are themselves made possible, of course, by the advent of language. The theorem regarding the evolution of *Homo sapiens* that strikes me as the most significant, most radical, most far-reaching, affirms that the process of generating, mastering, and transmitting true language societally and the process of transforming primate *homo sapiens* (the human infant) into a person — in large part, self-transformed — are one and the same. I tend to say, "generating" rather than "inventing," because we really have no clue as to what the crucial phases of evolution must have been like. It's a plausible "hypothesis" we have no inkling how to confirm or disconfirm.

The "three paradoxes" presuppose the heterodoxy just mentioned, but they also lead at once to the exploration of some of the central puzzles encountered in defining the human form of life. I'm particularly pleased with the unforced fluency and aptness of the resolution of each paradox and the force of their converging lessons regarding larger, programmatic decisions affecting well-known philosophical contests. The *Lectures* begin obliquely, each with its own puzzle, without betraying their eventual convergent unity: the paradoxes prove to be strategically placed, not doctrinally "cooked" in any troubling way; and, as we proceed from one to another, we find (I trust) that we've provisionally marked out what may be fairly regarded as the key notions involved in distinguishing and reinterpreting the essential contrast between physical nature and the humanly transformed world: that's to say, the essential categories of person, language, form of life of societies of enlanguaged, encultured persons. What becomes increasingly clear is the executive importance of the initial "correction" of evolutionary theory itself. The theorem (so to say) that impresses me here is the surprising reasonableness of treating the physical sciences as restrictive idealizations within the larger and more complex idiom and space of the human sciences and practical life itself, as opposed to the more familiar idea of construing the language of the human sciences as looser, often arbitrary attenuations and extensions of the supposedly adequate vocabulary of the physical sciences. The unity of science may, of course, still be supported here, but it will have been profoundly altered in its claims. I should perhaps add that the Michael Eldridge Lecture, for the Central European Pragmatism Forum (CEPF), 2016, proved to be a satisfactory free-standing confirmation of the need to acknowledge a coherent account of "collective individuals" in any would-be adequate treatment of the moral/political questions of our day. Sheer serendipity!

Finally, along related lines, the four lectures conspire to provide strong briefs on a number of the most important contests among currently competing philosophical "movements." I have the following issues in mind particularly: the confrontation between Kantian and pragmatist treatments of the essential problems of First Philosophy; an assessment of the tenability of a revival of rationalism in our time — ranging over Cartesian, Kantian, and (now, especially) Fregean lines (which, of course, may well depart from their eponymous sources); the changing status (that is, the constructivist nature) of the realism question; the parity and inseparability of experience and thought in epistemology; the futility of an autonomous semantics of any kind; prospects for a perspicuous revision of what to count as pragmatism now; and the appraisal of supposed affinities between classic and revisionary pragmatisms and, say, the work of the "Pittsburgh School," Wittgenstein, Kant himself, and others said to be pragmatists of a vanguard sort. Here, I confess my own pragmatist convictions and venture, very briefly, a few personal conclusions on the issues mentioned: in particular, that Kantianism and pragmatism appear to be irreconcilable; that Kantian and Fregean rationalisms are inherently regressive and more than difficult to validate; and that such vulnerabilities are clearly present in the rationalist ventures of the "Pittsburghers."

These last remarks are intended to be little more than a summary of what became, for me, the most provocative saliences of the talks themselves: for instance, that they are centered on the philosophical significance of the life of the human infant and that they are rightly read as post-Darwinian. But I would much rather like to believe that readers will find these talks both clear and agreeable, without the need of any prompting or promises for the future.

J. M.
December 2016

1.
PERSONS AS NATURAL ARTIFACTS

I

The hero of these lectures is the human primate: that's to say, the human infant, who, by its native, seemingly meager prelinguistic gifts, masters, easily and quickly, any and every natural language as a first language and, in doing that, transforms itself metaphysically (so to say) into the uniquely hybrid artifactual creature we name "person" or "self," signifying thereby the mastery of certain novel, utterly unmatched reflexive powers of thought and agency that mark the extraordinary career of the human race. We find ourselves confronted by a thoroughly naturalistic, encultured discontinuity within a palpable biological continuum of animal and human evolution, an anomaly that presages the all-too-hasty disjunctions of mind and body, thought and world, nature and spirit, law and history, invariance and flux, and the promise and limitations of the physical and human sciences that have bedeviled Western philosophy through the whole of its history.

In a word, philosophy and science — all truth-seeking disciplines — find themselves obliged to confirm their coherence and adequacy in terms of accommodating matters of fact akin to the judgment I've just tendered. I mean: philosophies of mind and enlanguaged culture must make sense of the evolutionary conditions under which what may be called the "external" and "internal" *Bildung* of the human race (the bridge roles, respectively, of successive species of the genus *Homo* and successive cohorts of the infant members of *Homo sapiens*); they must explain the original creation of language and the normal development of the human person. Academic philosophy is largely opposed to such inquiries. The enterprise remains conjectural, of course, even question-begging, once we confront the puzzles of the paleoanthropological evidence that informs us about the powers of the mature primate members of any of the species of *Homo* or of the cognitive import of the phased invention and mastery of language. Thus, one acknowledged authority on "the history of human thinking," Michael Tomasello, speculating on the unique distinctions of intelligence

manifested by *Homo sapiens*, in accord with the views of "a small group
of philosophers of action" (Tomasello's phrasing: intended to feature his
agreement with familiar figures like John Searle), has recently affirmed
that

> humans are able to coordinate with others, in a way that other primates
> seemingly are not, to form a "we" that acts as a kind of plural agent to create
> everything from a collaborative hunting party to a cultural institution.[1]

Tomasello, I suggest, has not thought carefully enough about the security
concerns of elephant families committed to thwarting the affectionate
kidnapping of baby elephants by rival families, or the coordinated hunting
of lion sisters, or the deliberate sieges of African farms by baboon cohorts;
and, of course, though oddly, he fails to feature the meaning of the
achievement of language itself, which would have obliged him (and us)
to justify the problematic demarcation between primate- and person-level
skills.

By and large, this is a neglected matter among linguists and primatologists
alike. Still, at least one small finding seems reasonably clear: Tomasello
has too low an opinion of the "we" capacities of non-human mammals; he
discounts too easily the intelligence of animals and he does not examine
closely enough the meaning of the hard-won achievement of the human
infant. The lesson I suggest we ponder is no more than this: natural
language may be, at least on the sparest of evidence, an exclusively human
achievement — an invention in some important measure (admittedly
unexplained), not an original biological gift of any kind (*pace* Chomsky);
not a "mental organ" (say) biologically evolved or somehow genetically
contrived. It's an achievement that, in the last analysis, is the *recto* side
of the self-transformation of the primate members of *Homo sapiens* into
persons (arguably, of *Neanderthalensis* and other barely glimpsed species
as well). Most important, its distinctive features answer always to the
startling fact that, as cultural artifacts, persons can claim no natural niche
or *telos* in the world they share with animals — animals, compellingly
fitted (though unwittingly) to some normatively enabling environment.

Human languages, I say, must be distinctly and conveniently flexible,
in order to accommodate (as we discover) *whatever* continually invented
novel ways of living in, and transforming, the world happen to mark the

---

1   Michael Tomasello, *A Natural History of Human Thinking* (Cambridge: Harvard
     University Press, 2014), p. 3. Compare John Searle, *The Construction of Social
     Reality* (New York: Free Press, 1995).

human career. My point is no more than that language and personhood defeat any chiefly biological model of evolution: man is a hybrid creature, mingling biologically and culturally acquired abilities, and the race itself must continually offset its penchant for fixity (both practical and theoretical) in a rapidly changing world. It seeks to preserve the functionality of ordinary language, by compromising with its seeming adequacy and precision, wherever its shortcuts and knowing inexactitudes appear benign enough and even advantageous. It tolerates a considerable measure of vagueness, error, indeterminacy, distortion, openness to diffuse usage, diversity, inconsistency, contradiction, inexactitude, vacuity, and sheer ignorance; at the same time it pursues all the forms of precision, accuracy, strict conditions of truth and validity that it can muster. The first of these functional competencies I name "mongrel language": I believe our survival requires its distinctive contribution, and therefore regard it as a profound mistake (memorably, Wittgenstein's, in the *Investigations*) to think that the rational progress of our form of life (and language) requires the gradual elimination of mongrel and philosophical intuition. (I shall come back to this concession.)

But is Tomasello speaking of the *primate* creature (*homo sapiens*) — as, explicitly, he seems to affirm — or the enlanguaged transform (of human primates) that we call a "person"? His own allies have no access to mature prelinguistic human primates of any kind — nor does he, nor do we. There *are* no such creatures to encounter now, even if we concede the familiar stalemate that accompanies speculations about "wild children." Tomasello does not answer: he cannot answer — on the strength of his own resources. There is no way to distinguish primate from person except by subtractive conjecture *from* whatever *we* now concede to be given by the acquisition of language. If we grant the conceptual and cognitive gap that Tomasello himself affirms between the great apes and man (as we now encounter *Homo sapiens* — that is, ourselves), then it's entirely reasonable to concede *both* that language is decisive for the formation of persons as well as for the fully determinate self-referential competences uniquely confined to *Homo sapiens* (if indeed they are uniquely manifested by humans) *and* that prelinguistic man was undoubtedly gifted (beyond the considerable, though still prelinguistic, communicative powers of the great apes) in some way that favored the initial onset of the invention of language.

Nevertheless, the putative "we"-agent of which Tomasello speaks — which Searle and Margaret Gilbert and Raimo Tuomela (and similar-minded philosophers of diverse convictions) casually endorse — appears on both sides of the primate/person divide, though in very different guises. The fatal error appears already in George Mead's classic analysis. Hence, what Tomasello says is trivially true on the language side and importantly mistaken on the prelinguistic side. Mead, of course, was unable to decide whether his dialectical use of the "I"/"me" schema modeled the functioning of well-formed persons *or* modeled no more than the enabling primate conditions leading *to* the very formation of persons. It's an extraordinary fact that Mead's confusion has been elevated to the rank of an essential resolution of the definitional question; in Mead's hands, the engine of the transformation rests with the acquired ability of humans to adopt the role of the "generalized other" — the source of Tomasello's and Searle's "we." But languageless apes and monkeys already show an ability to cooperate meaningfully, applying what they have learned (societally, culturally) without, yet, becoming persons. They lack language, but they possess "perceptual concepts"; and if they use such concepts intelligently and cooperatively, how can they be denied a capacity for *judgment*? I don't deny that *we* find it difficult to spell out the precise structure of animal judgment in a fine-grained way, though its general functionality tends to be clear enough. (We proceed here, of course, along anthropocentric lines. But that's a subsidiary matter.) I also believe that human infants must rely on perceptual concepts in learning discursive concepts. (I shall return to this).[2]

Mead characteristically fails to mark the strong disjunction, within the career of the species, of the functionalities of primate and person (and the reason for their all but ineluctable evolutionary sequence). In this sense, as we shall see, the concept of "self" or "person" is something of a mystery — in a way that suggests the relativization of the "actuality" of persons at

---

2   John McDowell's Kantianism has led him to make no more than some very tentative concessions in the direction of perceptual concepts; but he insists that animals are incapable of *judgment* — judgment, for McDowell, is thoroughly "discursive" (enlanguaged). I say rather that, although perception need not be perceptual judgment, concepts (of any kind) are plausibly and paradigmatically ascribed (in general and, certainly, in the Kantian sense) in contexts of operative judgment: hence, to admit (or, not to deny explicitly) something of the nature of perceptual concepts to animals is to admit (or not to deny explicitly) something of the nature of operative judgment to animals. The evidence challenges McDowell's artful compromise. A considerable run of current analytic treatments of the concept/judgment divide (regarding languageless animals) is usefully addressed in Carl Sachs, 'Resisting the Disenchantment of Nature: McDowell and the Question of Animal Minds', *Inquiry*, 55, 131–147. I'm persuaded that McDowell's stand in the *Woodbridge Lectures* is untenable — but then, so, too, is Kant's position, in the first *Critique*.

different levels or registers of mastering discourse. This allows for a more charitable reading of Descartes's *Cogito* than Descartes himself provides — which is, also, more stubborn, conceptually, than anything canonical rationalism could possibly confirm. Hence, I regard the admission of rationality to be entirely compatible with advanced animal life (viewed species-wise), though enlanguaged thought *is*, trivially, and momentously, confined to enlanguaged persons. Elephants, I suggest, are capable of elephantine rationality nevertheless, *in* cognition and understanding and conception and deed; they don't "think" as we think, though *we* ourselves are puzzled by our own ability as well as that of elephants.

You may protest that I've neglected animal "languages": the "language" of the honey bees, for instance, or that of dolphins or of whales. I acknowledge the disputed incipience, among chimpanzees and bonobos, of an elementary grasp of some dimension of human (natural) languages, as well as of proto-linguistic analogues of reference and predication among monkeys and apes. But I distinguish as forcefully as possible between linguistic and nonlinguistic communication, as with the semiotics of gestures (among wild dogs, that lack language) and humans (who have language). I'm prepared to yield ground wherever the evidence may require. But, thus far, I see no need to yield much ground, and I mean to resist obscuring the theory of persons.

It's in this spirit that I claim that our best guess at an answer holds that, whatever incipiencies approaching the determinate reflexive awareness of "oneself" *qua* self may be thought to arise among unlanguaged animals, the determinacy of the paradigmatic self is assuredly inseparable from the mastery of language, is in fact an essential part of what, precisely, we master in mastering a fully developed natural language. I'm entirely willing, I should add, to concede that the very notion of a "self" may well have begun, theoretically, as a thin artifactual (even fictional — grammatically fictional) construct of an abstractly functional sort that only gradually acquires (through continual use) the irresistibly practical sense and force of a thick and actual entitative identity. So that when Tomasello ventures his "shared intentionality hypothesis," which he characterizes as a sort of "we"-intentionality, he must be fudging (innocently, I would say, though not unlike Mead) between pre- and post-linguistic speculation.[3] In any case, the intentional nature of acts performed by the great apes do indeed approach, incipiently, the feats of persons, without entailing the reflexive conjectures of the self itself. That threatens to count as an

---

3   See Tomasello, *A Natural History of Human Thinking*, Ch. 1.

insoluble paradox for rationalists who insist on the discursivity of concepts (John McDowell, for instance.)

Of course, the matter is profoundly contested. More than that, the strictly biological evidence seems to confirm the cognitional (nativist) gap between the human primate and the great apes: it cannot, as matters now stand, confirm the continuum of the human and the animal without confirming as well the gap between the prelinguistic cognitive powers of ape and man that would explain (in some measure) both the absence of true language among the apes and the unique ability of the human infant to master any natural language at all from a languageless vantage. I leave room here, also, for the surmise (which I confess I find neither implausible nor unattractive), namely, that the linguistically exceptional bonobo Kanzi seems to have mastered — recognitionally, perhaps more than productively, but productively enough (so it has been plausibly claimed) — distinctly advanced linguistic skills, without explicit training: grammatically dependent clauses, for instance, and reference to the intentions and actions of other agents (whether bonobos or humans) not actually present (to ensure intended reference) in witnessed discursive episodes.[4] But if this be admitted — Tomasello is impressed, Chomsky is not — then Kanzi must be at least a-more-than-barely-incipient person; and, in conceding that much, we signal the ontologically contested nature of the self and the vagaries of linguistic incipience.

It's entirely reasonable to suppose that there are unique biological capabilities on the part of the human primate that provide a proper foundation for the infant's skill in mastering language, without supposing that the reflexive powers of selves or persons are themselves completely entailed in such capacities. Most discussants are reluctant to advocate the thesis that the posit of the self as the determinate site of speech acts and (other) deliberate or intended acts (enabled by language) may be the artifactual but substantialized minimal outcome of an originally practical

---

4   See Michael Tomasello and Josep Call, *Primate Cognition* (Oxford: Oxford University Press, 1997). My sense is that Tomasello has strengthened his impression of Kanzi's (and other apes') ability to discern the intentions of bonobos and familiar humans; we cannot be entirely sure that the seeming limitations in Kanzi's use of language may not be an artifact of the conditions of testing and training: the matter is not entirely clear. See, further, E.Sue Savage-Rumbaugh, *Ape Language* (New York: Columbia University Press, 1986); and E.Sue Savage-Rumbaugh *et al.*, 'Language Comprehension in Ape and Child', *Monographs of the Society for Research in Child Development*, 58 (3–4), no. 233; also, Michael Tomasello, *Origins of Human Communication*, (Cambridge: MIT Press, 2008), Chs. 6–7 (taken together).

(or grammatical) nominalization on our own part (in theorizing about the self). In any case, the matter inevitably challenges standard evolutionary theory, even where it exceeds or corrects the general lines of Darwin's original account: say, among the so-called "philosophical anthropologists" (Helmuth Plessner and his associates and allies), who were still inclined to conflate the conceptual difference between primate and person[5] — as does George Mead among the classic pragmatists, John Searle among the "we-intentionalists," and Tomasello among the primatologists. Because, if (as I'm persuaded) the self *is* the artifactual, though entirely naturalistic posit of the unified site of human thought and agency, then canonical evolutionary theory cannot possibly account for the standard forms of human development, without treating the evolution of the human being in hybrid, intertwined biological and enlanguaged (cultural) terms, that appear not to apply in the same way to other advanced animals. Viewed this way, it's as reasonable (possibly more reasonable) to regard the most fundamental physical sciences as disciplines *abstracted* and *idealized from the prior space* of the *human* sciences and practical life, as (or, than) it is to regard the inquiries of the human sciences and practical life as *extensions* or modifications (of some sort) *of* the foundational inquiries and language of the physical sciences. (I draw your attention, in passing, to the important grammatical liberty, or initial trickery, involved in fixing the reference — is it a merely mongrel reference? — to selves, which I return to in my second lecture.)

Here, I emphasize two caveats: one, that there can be no doubt that the invention or achievement of a natural language, which I take to be essentially a cultural feat open to natively gifted creatures — rather than an entirely unlearned, possibly minor genetic modification of the wiring of the brain, that somehow yields a "mental organ" whose functionality manifests itself instantly as linguistic — cannot possibly have been realized without enabling *prelinguistic* competences, either evolutionary (in the biological sense), at least partially encultured, or in the form of transformative, socially learned, socially transmitted, *cultural* improvements of *Homo sapiens*'s native powers, even if shared (up to a point) with the great apes themselves; and, the second caveat, that it is unquestionably true that the primate *preconditions* of *Homo sapiens*'s

---

5   For a reasonable summary of the "philosophical anthropologists'" inability or unwillingness to define the difference between primate and person, see Marjorie Grene, 'People and Other Animals', *The Understanding of Nature: Essays in the Philosophy of Biology* (Dordecht: D. Reidel, 1974), pp. 346–360, particularly p, 358.

gradual invention of language must include *pre*-personal, *proto*-personal, *ur*-personal stages of development that finally issue in paradigmatically person-level manifestations that may be difficult to distinguish clearly and determinately within the terms of a hybrid revision of the evolutionary continuum of the human primate and human person. My conjecture has it that *if* discursive concepts (problematically defined as "rational") are (or are largely) artifactual, then it is well-nigh impossible to deny the existence of perceptual and other nonlinguistic concepts.

The truth is, we are unable to sort these resemblant forms in an entirely explicit way, in good part because the theory of mind is so remarkably primitive (whether psychologically or rationally described), spanning, say, Descartes's self-thwarting conjectures and those of current speculation. I do hold, however, that the enabled powers of normative ordering and of confirming the identity and reidentification of individuated things (*under different descriptions*) exceed any pre-personal primate competence. I see no reason to suppose we cannot gain considerable conceptual ground — in distinguishing between primate and person — by adding to such discoveries. True language itself, I urge, is inseparable from the formation of persons. My premise, you remember, is, precisely, that the societal invention of language and the individual mastery of language effectively constitute the same process that we reasonably characterize as the transformation of the human primate into a person; and that Darwinian models of evolution fail to account for the full emergence (and uniquely enlanguaged powers) of the human being — because they fail to acknowledge the inherent inadequacy of any merely biological theory to account for paradigmatic persons, and because they fail to interpolate the requisite capacities (call them intelligent, rational — in a species-specific sense -, and conceptual — though nondiscursive — on the part of the human infant), adequate for "internal *Bildung*." We cannot, I submit, solve the puzzle of the human mode of being without conceding the depth of the conceptual revision of evolutionary theory that's still needed.

It's in this sense that I say the formation of persons is, effectively, a "metaphysical" change, a change of being, meaning (by that) a change so profound that we exceed the explanatory resources of the whole of material biology — in any sense confined to chemical or biochemical or genetic or epigenetic or standard explanations by purely physical or causal means. I suggest that the description and explanation of linguistic activity, however biologically enabled, cannot be given in biological or, for that matter, in languageless behavioral terms alone: what's required is, in fact, profoundly incommensurable (though not incompatible) with physicalist discourse.

There's an important clue buried in this casual acknowledgement that I shall return to, bearing, of course, on the matter of "mongrel" language. But what I wish to emphasize particularly is the conjectural nature of the entire matter. My own intuition is committed to the thesis that personhood and natural language are radically novel developments, biologically and culturally inseparable "aspects" of the same "evolutionary" turn, that may well be unique to the human race (or to some small cluster of races that, except for ours, which seems to have been hybridized, have gone extinct). I begin with the entwinement of biology and culture (or "mind"); others — Chomsky, most notably, begin with genetics and the computational functionality of the brain. At the moment there's a democratic sparsity of strategically placed information adequate to discern the inevitability of any presently contrived theory. It's entirely possible that better answers will have to conjure (finally) with the mind/body problem: that is, with the meaning of "emergent" and the extension of the "physical." But that confirms again the naïve standing of the present state of play.

Let me say, by way of a provisional summary, that the infant's intelligence must include prelinguistic *conceptual* capacities (*if* discursive conceptual capacities are conceded to be socially acquired as well as essential in the successful mastery of language itself); and if that's true, then we already have reasonably strong grounds for conjecturing that languageless animals of high intelligence may be characterized as rational creatures (in the species-specific sense), as possessing perceptual and experiential concepts (akin to those of the human infant, I should add), in virtue of which we cannot fail to attribute to them (on empirical grounds) — however anthropomorphized — powers akin to consciousness, inference, thinking, judgment, knowledge, confirmation, commitment, decision, and the like.

The human infant must be uniquely endowed within the evolutionary continuum of animal and human nature; and a phenomenology of the mental must be applicable, analogically, in *theorizing* about primate and nonprimate perception and experience, as well as at the level of human reportage. There is no other way to explain the bridge role of the human infant in understanding the achievement of enlanguaged persons. I emphasize the conjectural liberty we avail ourselves of here, largely because of the nearly Cartesian nature of recent applications of the Kantian treatment of discursive rationality and discursive conception: notably in the extreme — repeatedly affirmed but hardly defended — "Kantian" reading of human intelligence advocated by John McDowell — in his *Woodbridge Lectures* and in his seeming (still extreme rationalist) "correction" of the Woodbridge Lectures, in, for instance, his essay, *Avoiding the Myth of the*

Given.[6] But I must also mention in the same breath the effective omission of the *conceptual* powers of infants and animals in (to my mind) the more important, more fine-grained, more accurate and compelling account of the discursive treatment of rationality, conception, and consciousness (among enlanguaged persons) spelled out (along Husserlian phenomenological lines) by, for instance, Dan Zahavi.

Zahavi's argument appears in his *Mindedness, Mindlessness, and First-Person Authority*, which convincingly exposes the excessive claims of both McDowell and Hubert Dreyfus (in their well-known "debate" on the nature of the mental).[7] I shall treat these discussions as symptoms of a residual Cartesianism (however innocently betrayed) that both McDowell and Zahavi (and nearly all contemporary discussants of the matter) share, as in the general use of the term "*non*conceptual" to signify (without disjunction) both (say) phrases like "nonconceptual content" (as in the Kantian sense of distinguishing "sensibility" and "thinking" discursively) and what (contrary to Kant's and Husserl's usage) might have been defended in terms of the distinction between linguistic or enlanguaged concepts and specifically perceptual and experiential concepts that are either entirely prelinguistic or are conjoined with, or integrated into, discursive concepts. I take what I've already said — about the bridge role of human infants and the intelligence of the most advanced animals — that it must be a mistake to claim that prelinguistic infants (*a fortiori*, unlanguaged animals) must lack altogether the use of nondiscursive concepts that appear to be essential to the abilities we cannot rightly deny them (on the empirical evidence).

I'm persuaded that we cannot make sense of the abilities we attribute to humans who normally master speech, if we deny them the use of nondiscursive concepts. But, of course, the mere admission of nondiscursive concepts stalemates Kant's entire invention.

In any case, I see no way to explain discursive concepts if there are no perceptual or experiential concepts to build on. How could we possibly explain coming to understand the meanings of words and sentences? There's the strongest clue regarding the philosophical relevance of the Darwinian and post-Darwinian discoveries. McDowell's theory (in the Woodbridge

6   The *Woodbridge Lectures* appear in final form in John McDowell, *Having the World in View: Essays on Kant, Hegel, and Sellars* (Cambridge: Harvard University Press, 2009), Pt. I, pp. 3–65; *Avoiding the Myth of the Given* appears in the same volume, at pp. 256–272.

7   See Dan Zahavi, *Mindedness, Mindlessness, and First-Person Authority*, in Joseph K. Shear (ed.) *Mind, Reason, and Being-in-the-World: The McDowell-Dreyfus Debate* (London: Routledge, 2013), pp. 320–343.

Lectures) counts among the most uncompromisingly Kantian approaches to the conceptual issue that must be addressed. From the start, Zahavi's treatment is simply restricted to the discursive form of rationality, though he gives the impression that he's speaking of concepts in unrestrictedly universal terms. That cannot possibly be true.

II

I find it entirely plausible to construe an infant's ability to point meaningfully (in contexts of societal instruction or rearing), as both intentional and communicative, while remaining entirely prelinguistic. Laboratory apes have been taught to master human pointing as well; but that alone does not *confirm* that apes engage in discourse or are already persons. Tomasello confirms that apes in the wild also point intentionally. If so, then he defeats his own conjecture. I have already conceded that the solidarity of elephant troupes, baboon sieges of South African farmhouses, female lions hunting together among antelope show definite signs of learned planning and cooperation ("we"-intentionality, as Tomasello has it), without inventing or mastering or even requiring language — and, of course, without functioning as selves. Hence, when an "evolutionary anthropologist" like Tomasello declares: "Language is the capstone of uniquely human thinking, not the foundation",[8] I find it perfectly reasonable (though potentially confusing) to agree with him wherever he is able to demonstrate that there are (say) uniquely human biological gifts (or gifts modified by socially contrived *pre*linguistic learning) that we take to contribute to laying a proper ground for the invention and mastery of language (or something akin); but I believe Tomasello nonetheless fails to come to terms with the thesis of the artifactual nature of persons, *within* the bounds of the hybrid intertwining of biological and cultural forces that yield no more than *prelinguistic* (though still distinctly semiotic) gains: the gains of prelinguistic infants, for instance, approaching some first steps in learning a language. I'm persuaded that Tomasello's own thesis — "the so-called shared intentionality, or 'we' intentionality thesis" (his own expression), which, as I say, Tomasello appears to share with theorists like John Searle and Margaret Gilbert — takes the confused, or equivocal form of mingling primate- and person-level expressions. For his part, Searle tends to endow *his* human primates with nearly all the essential capacities

---

8   Tomasello, *A Natural History of Human Thinking*, p. 127.

of evolved persons: the invention and mastery of language is therefore not a problem for him. Tomasello does not go that far, but he fails to explain the difference nonetheless.

But if this much is true, then I, for one, am prepared to concede cognitive powers to advanced, though languageless, animals — including the "use" of nonlinguistic analogues of inference, judgment, evidentiary confirmation and the like. Nevertheless, the discursive modeling of such processes cannot be more than heuristic, as we now understand animal intelligence. If you acknowledge Kanzi's achievements, then the bonobos may occupy a range of functioning comparable to that of the transitional powers of very young children beginning to acquire a language. If you allow the argument, then, I daresay, Kanzi and the human infant bring us to the edge of defeating Darwin and Kant (*a fortiori*, contemporary Kantians and Husserlians like McDowell and Zahavi) in the same breath.

Broadly speaking, any acceptable reconciliation of the opposed pairings I've begun with — mind and body, thought and world, law and history, and the rest — within the bounds of nature, without foundational or normative privilege of any kind, construing all such dualities coherently and consistently, preserving the continuum of animal and human powers, counts, in most of the idioms of the new millennium's philosophies, certainly in my own intrusive ideology, as thoroughly pragmatist in sweep, or at least as compatible or companionable with same. My thought is that this presumption may very well define the most promising, most arresting philosophical ventures of our age. In any event, I confess I start from this corner of the world and find myself entirely open to provisional, selective, and functional recruitments (in terms of pragmatist affinities) among initially alien or opposed figures and doctrinal proposals that would have seemed impossible to countenance a short while ago: for instance, regarding Descartes, Leibniz, Hume, Kant, Fichte, Hegel, Nietzsche, Frege, Peirce, Russell, Husserl, Heidegger, Merleau-Ponty, Carnap, Quine, Strawson, Davidson, Sellars, and Wittgenstein at the very least. By and large, these are the salient figures I find I must conjure with especially — that is, genealogically, *not* in any way to prejudge the merit or importance of any of their contributions. But then, to suggest that there may be pragmatist affinities between such figures and the classic pragmatists will no longer seem odd.

Furthermore, *if* prelinguistic infants actually learn the remarkably complex languages that they do, then that already yields a more than plausible reason to think that language must preserve a relatively simplified channel of mongrel discourse (a kind of *lingua franca* or creole, within any home language), to ensure quotidian fluency — which, nevertheless, also enables progress in the direction of whatever complexities any viable home language is bound to introduce children, strangers (and others) to. It's my contention that the analysis of our quotidian world (the world of persons) is probably too difficult for man to fathom quickly or better than he fathoms any part of physical nature, to yield up the opportunistic instrumentalities of the verbal evasions, elisions, vacuities, compromises, doubtful nominalizations, even benign falsities of the mongrel discourse he learns to live with. Just try, for instance, to state clearly and simply what thinking is — supposing (always) that we do think! It seems we cannot function in ordinary life (as the rationalists suppose we can) if we must rely in some significant measure (as I suggest we must) on the admittedly risky resources of mongrel discourse — that's to say, with all the familiar imperfections of ordinary language that we blithely accommodate. Cultural infancy surrounds us forever: I shall try to show, shortly (in the briefest way), that both Wittgenstein and Frege were profoundly mistaken at the very outset of their superb but irreconcilably opposed philosophical contributions regarding the adequacy of ordinary discourse.

Let me collect the summary force of the single premise I've begun with here, before proceeding further. I mean: the easy confirmation of the human infant's ability to master natural language and to take up its intended function as an apt member of a society of mature persons, who already share a language and a culture. To admit the human infant's empirical achievement — I call it empirical rather than innate or transcendental — is, I say, to implicate the impossibility of accounting for the emergence of the integral human being (as we characterize ourselves) in evolutionary terms wherever the story is strictly confined to biological processes alone (in effect, in accord with the defects and omissions of Darwin's original vision and neo-Darwinian enlargements). But to admit that much reminds us of the strategic importance of perceptually and experientially grounded concepts (accessible to human infants and nonhuman animals alike, in their respective ways, *if* concepts are admitted at all, within the continuum of canonical evolution).

I add at once — opportunistically, though for good reason — that this single admission exposes a mortal weakness in Descartes's and Kant's (and, indeed, in all classic rationalist) theories of cognition, *of both* metaphysical and methodological sorts and reminds us (thereby) of the ultimate good sense of a cognate part of Aristotle's "metaphysics" of cognition (hence, of concepts laxer than the linguistic or discursive). For it may indeed be true — I take it to be true — that even the so-called mastery of "rational" (or enlanguaged) concepts (think, here, of "pure" and "applied" or "impure" arithmetic and geometric concepts, in the setting of Cartesian, Kantian, and Fregean speculation) may well depend on the enabling mastery of perceptual and agentive fluencies, even where putatively "pure" concepts appear to have no direct conceptual entanglement with perceptual concepts — granting, always, of course, that there *are* concepts and that many animal species are capable of high intelligence: as in inference, memory, learning, invention, skill, instruction of the young, judgment, purposive behavior — in effect, in forms of rationality "below" (as we say) the level of linguistic competence.

There is, in fact a remarkably instructive passage excerpted from Wilfrid Sellars's *Empiricism and the Philosophy of Mind*, that Robert Brandom interprets along decidedly rationalist lines, that draws conviction, loosely, from jointly Kantian and Fregean sources, and that marks the resurgence (post-Rorty) of rationalism in our time, as itself a form of pragmatism. I mean the somewhat muffled (various) rationalisms of the so-called "Pittsburgh School" (to include Brandom, Sellars, John McDowell, and, by courtesy, Richard Rorty), which, chiefly advanced by Brandom and Sellars, attempt to link in a fresh way Kantian and Fregean variants of the rationalist vision. That precise maneuver — which obliquely recalls Rudolf Carnap's (Frege's student's) related gesture during the positivist surge in the early decades of the twentieth century — is both alluring and difficult to isolate as genuinely autonomous in a way that might compare favorably with Frege's own treatment of mathematical reasoning in his *Begriffsschrift*: a matter more obscurely bruited in Sellars's early forays and reclaimed (never more than programmatically) by Brandom. (I'll come to the passage in a moment.)

But it's also meant to strengthen our sense of "discovering" laxer rational rigors of justified judgment regarding the normative "methodological framework" of reasoning, potentially among any and all inquiries, including the work of the human sciences and practical life, beyond any merely hit-or-miss search for first-order empirical evidence. I find a collision of motives here, that stamps the projects of these newly minted rationalists (Kantians or Fregeans) of our own day, who envision a fusion or reorientation of pragmatism involving distinctly Fregean options. Their ventures need to be reappraised — though, frankly, I regard them, at best, as heuristic (when viewed as ideal possibilities) more than as evidentiarily reliable (if actually applied in the real world). The intended rationalist precision trails off into undeniable vagueness in Sellars's treatment and appears as something of a mongrel intrusion in Brandom's open admission that (as yet) we cannot support claims firmer than suggestive analogies (as with AI simulation).

Here, in a distinctly candid moment, Brandom goes to some lengths to qualify the would-be rationalist grounding of his own inferentialism — in particular, his version of "material inference" (Wilfrid Sellars's term). He says, for instance, that "autonomous discursive practices *essentially* and not just *accidentally* involve...at least some material [that is, 'nonlogical' — non-formal] inferences"; that they "must [also] have some vocabulary that can be used *observationally*, in reliably differentially elicited noninferential reports," that pertinently bear on the appraisal of "materially good and materially bad inferences" (Brandom's wording). Furthermore, and most important, Brandom concedes that, "material inference is in general *nonmonotonic*," that is, "*defeasible*, by [reference to] collateral circumstances that thereby count as special [disciplines, *not* actually algorithmic or rule-governed or nomological: medicine, law, the human sciences, say, contrasted with 'formal logical systems', mathematical reasoning, and thoroughly mathematized physics perhaps]."

Brandom speaks here of "special sciences" (medicine, say) because, although they are "defeasible," such disciplines are not completely determinate or closed in the way of applied rules or criteria or *ceteris paribus* clauses, by which their apparent claims, conjectures, and judgments may be reliably defeated. These, then, provide instances of "material inference" (in Sellars's sense, coopted by Brandom), that are firmer than the quotidian inferences of ordinary pragmatic situations: so much so, I'm inclined to believe, that the latter tend to dwindle into uncertain disputations. Here, speaking loosely, "defeasibility" is a consideration that applies improvisationally, case-by-case; but, if so, there may be no point in collecting such cases if what we want is a degree of rigor of at least the sort found among the "special sciences" or something akin — or stronger. To put the point in the frankest way: the *Begriffsschrift* analogy loses persuasive force wherever our conception of what to count as material inference itself becomes quarrelsome, as, along observational and pragmatic lines, Brandom candidly concedes the point.

Roughly speaking, nonmonotonic inferences do not answer to any "definite totality of possible defeasors"; so-called *ceteris paribus* clauses mark "an unavoidable feature of ordinary material inference" and cannot be expected to convert the apparently nonmonotonic into the monotonic.[9]

---

9   Robert B. Brandom, *From Empiricism to Expressivism: Brandom Reads Sellars* (Cambridge: Harvard University Press, 2015), pp. 163–164.

All such constraints point, inexorably, to the ineliminable influence of perceptual, experiential, intentional and other psychological factors in appraising the relatively unruly nature of Brandom's (and Sellars's) would-be inferentialism, as being in any way a reasonable and sufficiently convincing analogue of Frege's mathematical reasoning.[10] This explains, in part, Brandom's motive for merging (in some measure) Kant's and Frege's very different purposes.[11]

But then, having made these good-faith concessions, Brandom turns the tables on the loose empiricist impulse of classic pragmatism, by isolating, as well as possible, the would-be *rationalist autonomy* of the inferentialism of the so-called "framework" of reasoning in *any* inquiry aspiring to scientific standing, that might compare favorably with the would-be autonomous (rational) rigor of arithmetic thinking (largely *à la* Frege). There's the regressive impulse that I espy; for there's a world of difference (certainly, after Frege) between the autonomy of, say, arithmetic reasoning about "pure" numbers (or, better, about functions and higher-level law-like relations among functions), possibly even extending to parts of mathematized physics — though Brandom is dubious. What I say here (and mean to support, however obliquely, in closing this lecture and opening the second) is that our acknowledging that the human person is an artifactual transform of the human primate and that the invention of language is, whatever else it may have become, a *mongrel*, motley, multifunctional instrument for effective survival among the things the human being claims to perceive and manipulate for its own purposes: an insuperably limiting constraint on the would-be autonomy of rational thinking at any level of inferentialist construction. The conjectured inferential ("metaphilosophical") structure of the "framework" (the logical space, so to say, of any well-ordered rational inquiry) is bound to be, I daresay, a Fregean-like self-deception if (as with Brandom) material inference is already acknowledged to be thoroughly nonmonotonic,[12] by

---

10   Compare Danielle Macbeth, *Realizing Reason: A Narrative of Truth and Knowing* (Oxford: Oxford University Press, 2014). especially Ch. 7.

11   For the briefest evidence of Brandom's view of Carnap's role in linking Kant's and Frege's rationalisms, see Brandom, *From Empiricism to Expressivism*, pp. 22–24. Brandom's conjectures about the Fregean themes of both Sellars and Carnap appear to rest on very slim grounds. See, also, for some oblique references to Carnap's and Wittgenstein's responses to Frege's logic, Daniel Macbeth, *Frege's Logic* (Cambridge: Harvard University Press, 2005), pp. 182–184 nn6–7. Macbeth does not pursue the Carnap connection in her *Realizing Reason*.

12   The most up-to-date defense that Brandom offers appears in *From Empiricism to Expressivism*, Ch.4. on the significance of Frege's mature conception of his own

and large quarrelsomely defeated or justified, and likely to be explained *ad hoc* and individually.

I must apologize for the heavy language here. (It's not my choice.) Nevertheless, one begins to see that the revival of Fregean rationalism — *a fortiori*, the much-too-easy union of Kantian and Fregean rationalisms (Brandom's temptation, which he finds embedded in Sellars's conjectures) — is ultimately regressive, certainly anti-Darwinian, not at all interested in the artifactuality of the human person or of natural language itself. The issue may seem alien at first, until you recall that Brandom believes he's fashioning a rationalist version of pragmatism, the intended ground of his proposed inferentialism — an "analytic pragmatism," as he calls it, partly based on his reading of Rorty and Sellars — meant to displace the executive role of the continuum of the animal and the human and the primacy of "experience" (at once animal and human), as they appear in both John Dewey's and Charles Peirce's accounts of the classic phase of pragmatism.

Turn back, then, to Sellars: Sellars's sentences (the ones in question, which Brandom cites) run as follows: the first,

> In the dimension of describing and explaining the world, science is the measure of all things, of what is that it is and of what is not that it is not. (§41)

the second,

> [In] characterizing an episode or a state as that of *knowing*, we are not giving an empirical description of that episode or state, we are placing it in the logical space of reasons, of justifying and being able to justify what one says. (§36)

Begriffsschrift — logically *and* philosophically. I'm very much in debt to Danielle Macbeth's *Realizing Reason* (already remarked) as well as her earlier, thoroughly convincing (more restricted) *Frege's Logic* (Cambridge: Harvard University Press, 2005), especially Chs. 2–3. Nevertheless, in acknowledging Frege's revolutionary conception of the "science of logic," I confess I'm not persuaded that there is a similar "pure" structure at the "metaphilosophical" level governing "material inference" among any familiar empirically or agentively (intentionally) qualified figures, such as Carnap, Sellars, Brandom, and (if I read her correctly) Macbeth are inclined to favor. I take the pros and cons of such extensions, however, to define one of the most strategically placed philosophical disputes of our age. If I understand the issue correctly, the question that remains asks whether there are Fregean "thoughts" that govern all truth-seeking inquiries. I suppose that there are not. (See *Frege's Logic*, §§4.5, 5.4). The upshot is that we remain constrained by the insuperable paradoxes of First Philosophy.

Brandom's gloss is instructive, even as it narrows the sense of what Sellars offers:

> The first passage [Brandom says], often called the *"scientia mensura,"* expresses a kind of scientific naturalism. Its opening qualification is important: there are [he warns us] other discursive and cognitive activities besides describing and explaining. The second passage says that characterizing something as a knowing is one of them. And indeed, Sellars means that in characterizing something even as a believing or a believable, as conceptually contentful at all, one is doing something other than describing it. One is placing the item in a normative space articulated by relations of what is a reason for what. Meaning, [for Sellars] is a normative phenomenon that does not fall within the descriptive realm over which natural science is authoritative.[13]

There's the fateful — and futile — argument: the authority of the thoroughly "rationalist" treatment of the inferentialist structure of the "framework" of any inquiry that rightly counts as "knowing" is indeed normative and, therefore, *not* descriptive (as remarked by both Sellars and Brandom), in spite of the fact that it *applies* to the descriptive materials of natural and human sciences and practical life in the large, and even in more informal inquiries (say, art criticism and historical interpretation). I cannot see the force of Brandom's (*a fortiori* Sellar's) maneuver, which is well on its way to becoming a distinctly fashionable option in current philosophical circles. But is it really viable? I venture to say (without meaning to change the thrust of the question) that Brandom's account may be even more anti-pragmatist (and regressive) than Rorty's post-modernist rebuttal.

It's precisely here (§36) that Sellars permits us to glimpse the unmarked "Fregean" themes that Brandom adopts in his own inferentialism: the escape from the reflexive *a priori* of epistemology, the dependence of the empirical sciences on a rationalist "metaphilosophical" platform, and the "Fregeanizing" of Kantianism itself. Rorty's charge maintains that pragmatism utterly fails wherever philosophy fails utterly; Brandom's charge (which is partly Rortyan) argues that classic pragmatism's empiricist inclination must be subordinated to the reclamation of pragmatism's rightful rationalist ground (*à la* Kant, Frege, or what may still be recovered

---

13   The sentences cited from Sellars appear in Wilfrid Sellars, *Empiricism and the Philosophy of Mind*, in *Science, Perception, and Reality* (London: Routledge & Kegan Paul, 1963), pp. 127–196. (The essay is published also as a separate volume, edited by Brandom, under the same title, with Harvard University Press, 1997.) Brandom's gloss appears in his *From Empiricism to Expressivism*, pp. 30–31.

from Carnap, Wittgenstein, and Sellars — but not, at least not readily, from figures like C.I. Lewis, Quine, and Davidson, or, for that matter, McDowell). Brandom characterizes the project as "programmatic." But I think that means that it need never be recovered as more than heuristic — which is to say, it remains effectively unsecured.

In any event, I see no way to explain the construction of a plausible "framework" argument (which Brandom hardly means to be a primal or privileged "foundation"), that may be viewed (instead) as a quasi-Fregean posit that enables us to see just how the natural sciences and the whole of practical reasoning may be brought back to their rationalist paradigm, without disallowing the play of dependent, non-inferential, empirical resources that count in important ways toward the realist success of our cognitive claims. There's the plan Brandom believes he shares with Sellars. The "framework" applies to an empirical domain (however narrowly or generously construed) without the need for any equilibration between its rationalist and empiricist premises and powers.

Something analogous is said to obtain in mathematics, in spite of the fact that mathematical entities do not belong to the empirical world. Put more frontally: I take Brandom's gloss to be — at the very least, intended to be — a proper analogue of Frege's mature reading of his own *Begriffsschrift*, applied (now) to the empirical and practical world (featuring the systematic primacy of material inference). I don't, however, find any compelling evidence that the analogy *holds*! I marvel at the *Begriffsschrift*'s achievement. I admit that theoretical physics is remarkably mathematized. I think we cannot refuse inferentialism an important place at the philosophical rostrum. I don't deny that the law of identity ($a = a$) is, "transparently," necessarily true. But the whole of the argument falls short of the mark in several decisive ways: for one thing, there's no real progress in demonstrating that pragmatic contexts must yield promisingly on the monotonicity matter; and, secondly, there seems to be no close-enough analogy between "metalinguistic" reasoning drawn (say), independently, from physics and from arithmetic.

You must bear in mind that "*to place an item* in a normative space" (as Sellars has it) *is* to place *it* (consulting doxastic or cognitive attributions that characteristically trigger nonmonotonic complications) in a decidedly uncertain — possibly unmanageable — inferential space. (Sellars is cannily silent here: Brandom is bolder, decidedly more voluble, distinctly more adventurous and unguarded.) In any case, I find no satisfactory argument in either Brandom or Sellars, or among their champions. In fact, Brandom himself emphasizes the chronic nonmonotonicity of "framework" speculations; Sellars effectively ducks the question. I mean the question, whether "rational" constraints on the "framework" of inferences within one or another science or practice of pragmatic know-how can be convincingly treated as free of any perceptual or experiential or cognitionally qualified agentive considerations. Brandom's admission of the nonmonotonicity of such inferences would seem to belie any supposed such autonomy.

I therefore take the argument to fail, and with it the thesis of the would-be primacy of inferentialism itself: Brandom's doctrine cannot deliver the resource it promises: it puts in question pragmatism's animal grip on what has come to be called the realist "friction" of perception and experience. If you add to this the effect of the self-referential paradoxes of epistemology, the informal, fluxive, tacit, and abductive complexities of cognition, you become aware again of the completely unearned assurances of any would-be alliance between Kantian and Fregean rationalism. You must see that I'm combating contemporary forms of rationalist regression in a post-Darwinian world. Hans Sluga pertinently reports that:

> Frege believed that arithmetic is necessary for the justification of scientific induction. It is also necessary [he claims] for the formulation of the more abstract empirical laws. To prove that arithmetic truths are *a priori* is therefore to prove not just that there are isolated pieces of *a priori* knowledge, but that *a priori* knowledge is fundamental to empirical knowledge.[14]

Nevertheless, we must ask ourselves: should Frege's conviction be dismissed in the same spirit in which Quine dismisses the comic futility of Peirce's effort to support his infinitist fallibilism by the arithmetic of infinitesimals? Does Thomas Kuhn's now more-or-less admired conception of discontinuous paradigm shifts among the natural sciences count as a decisive objection to the presumption of Fregean "Thoughts"? I believe it should. Bear in mind that, in a relatively late paper (1918–19), *The Thought: A Logical Inquiry*, Frege offers the following extraordinary claim:

> All sciences have truth as their goal; but logic is concerned with it in a quite different way from this. It has much the same relation to truth as physics has to weight or heat. To discover truths is the task of all sciences: it falls to logic to discern the laws of truth.[15]

---

14   Hans D. Sluga, *Gottlob Frege* (London: Routledge & Kegan Paul, 1980), p. 103.
15   Gottlob Frege, *The Thought: A Logical Inquiry*, trans. A.M. and M. Quinton, in E.D. Klemke (ed.) *Essays on Frege* (Urbana: University of Illinois Press, 1968), pp. 507–535, at p. 507.

Extraordinary invention! What could possibly be said in support of, or in opposition to, the "extension" of the Fregean paradigm within ordinary science?

Of course, *if* Frege could have made the doctrine convincing, the *a priori* "ground" of science would have been confirmed — or greatly strengthened. But is there any prospect of that? Here, the vulnerability of Frege's *a priori* more than matches the presumption of Kant's *a priori*. When, in *Making It Explicit*, Brandom qualifies his admiration for Wittgenstein's *Investigations*, by insisting that Wittgenstein was surely mistaken in denying that there *is* a "downtown" in a continually changing city — meaning by that metaphor, as I conjecture, that Wittgenstein failed to grasp the *Fregean* import of his own figurative comparison with the analysis of language (particularly, the analysis of language games) — he rides roughshod over Wittgenstein's more than dissatisfaction with what he (Wittgenstein) takes to be both Russell's and Frege's conceptual distortions.

I should perhaps also mention that it is relatively easy to see that Brandom largely follows Sellars in the latter's well-known, very early paper, *Language, Rules, and Behavior* (1949), in which Sellars is thinking of Frege's doctrine, but pursues it in application to what he seems to treat as Kant's anticipation of something akin to Frege's rigor; and yet Sellars does not (if I remember correctly) actually mention Frege in the paper, or offer more than an enthusiastic affirmation of a doctrine (in good part) close to the Fregean notion I've cited. Sellars attempts there to explicate what *he* means (I conjecture), reading Frege, or Kant with Frege in mind, when he says:

> The mode of existence of a rule is as a generalization written in flesh and blood, or nerve and sinew, rather than pen and ink. A rule, existing in its proper element, has the logical form of a generalization. Yet a rule is not *merely* a generalization which is formulated in the language of intra-organic process.... What do [the] special features in the formulation of rules indicate [that is, terms like "correct," "proper," "right"]? They give expression to the fact that a rule is an embodied generalization, which, to speak loosely but suggestively, tends to make itself true. Better, it tends to inhibit the occurrence of such events as would falsify it.[16]

This may well be the most Fregean of Sellars's papers, though you sense its oblique indecision. What Sellars has in mind is the idea that, normatively,

---

16   Wilfrid Sellars, *Language, Rules, and Behavior*, in *Pure Pragmatics and Possible Worlds: The Early Essays of Wilfrid Sellars*, ed, Jeffrey F. Sicha (Atascadero: Ridgeview, 1980, 2005), pp. 117–134, at p, 123.

the laws of "thought" (Fregean "thoughts") are the necessary rules of truth, but (also) that, if we treat them only empirically, they may be denied or defied — which we may override only if we actually grasp the rationalist function of the linguistic symbols we use in thinking "about *this* world in *every rule-regulated respect*":[17] that is, *a priori*, as necessarily true. As far as I can see, neither Sellars nor Brandom — nor Frege, nor Kant — fulfills the promise of the necessary laws of truth, which would yield something more than the hope that there must be an analogue of the main argument of the *Begriffsschrift* governing the sciences and ordinary discourse. I believe *that* to be a mistake: Sellars and Brandom have simply followed Frege over the philosophical cliff. The best advice seems to be to return to the more manageable, more rewarding empiricist or commonsense informalities of Peirce (which I collect under the terms of abductive reasoning) or even to the mythic terms (the less than perspicuous exuberance) of Dewey's and James's empiricisms. In any event, the connective argument, the rationalist argument, is plainly missing. No one can spell out the actual "metaphilosophical framework" — the analogue of the *Begriffsschrift* model — that may be shown to constrain all truth-seeking inquiries addressed to the actual world.

I reject the *scientia mensura* thesis as flatly false and unsupported by Sellars's own arguments. I have, elsewhere, shown that Sellars, effectively and fairly and against his own persuasion, undermines the likelihood that what he calls the "scientific image" will ever be able to replace (or eliminate) the conceptual vision of the so-called "manifest image" — in which such concepts as person, intentionality, normativity, language, and discursive cognition or judgment find their natural home.[18] We cannot do without these notions *and* they are obviously irreducible in their own right. (This single theme haunts all of my own arguments and begins to explain what, in the second lecture, I take up in the analysis of that all-important instrument we call ordinary discourse.)

If Sellars's argument favoring the "scientific image" over the "manifest image" fails, then Brandom's reading of the import of Sellars's "space of reasons" thesis also fails. There's a mortal gap in Brandom's brief, which,

---

17   Sellars, *Language, Rules, and Behavior*, pp. 123–124.
18   See Sellars, *Empiricism and the Philosophy of Mind*, p. 173. The argument appears in my *Reading Wilfrid Sellars's 'Philosophy and the Scientific Image of Man', with Robert Brandom at One's Side*, forthcoming in *Wilfrid Sellars: Idealism and Realism* ed. Patrick Reider, with Bloomsbury Press. I address Peirce's abductive alternative in my *Toward a Metaphysics of Culture* (London: Routledge, 2016), Ch. 3.

as far as I can see, Brandom nowhere fills successfully: it appears in different guises in Sellars and McDowell and haunts the whole of Western philosophy. The counter-consideration runs this way: that, although it's entirely reasonable to claim that normative disjunctions are not descriptive or explanatory, *their actual use* and application in the natural and human sciences and practical life characteristically require and presuppose the empirical world. (My own solution argues that if and when we place normativity within "the space of reasons," we *place* the space of reasons within the space of a "form of life"!)

In this sense, the extension of cognitive and rational abilities to languageless animals also warns us *not* to regard reason as a determinate cognitive "faculty" addressed, autonomously, to a "real" world (say, a world of numbers) *or* the "actual" world (*the* world we say we occupy and the sciences address — or, even more straitly, the actual world, completely enlanguaged). We must, therefore, make room, species-wise, for the rationality of animals.

My ultimate guess is that Kant was a less-than-secret member of the clan of rationalists he publicly opposed: that Frege was a reemboldened rationalist, with insufficient resources for extending the *Begriffsschrift* argument to broadly empirical or commonsense inquiries (as in the sciences and practical matters): that Sellars was a conflicted distant cousin of the rationalists, fashionably drawn to the Fregean option (perhaps by Carnap) but unable to confirm the common rationalism of Kant and Frege; that Brandom (somewhat poisoned by Rorty's destructive purism, but always his own man) simply commits himself heroically and impatiently to Frege, believing he will be able to provide a satisfactory premise in his own time — that is, so as to reinterpret the entire narrative of Western philosophy in accord with a suitable union of Fregean and Kantian rationalism that need not deny empiricism's diminished resources. Furthermore, I believe that what all this would require is likely to be much too much to believe possible — and, thus, to be ultimately regressive (not altogether unlike Kant's original strategy).

How, for instance, could the Fregean model, or the Kantian, be reconciled with the contingent artifactuality of the human person? Or, alternatively, what metaphilosophical necessities are we bound by, that could possibly disallow our relying on the salient vagaries of consensual experience — in favor of rationalism? I find no contest here. Canonically, pragmatism and rationalism are irreducibly opposed. Still, one hears it said, in our own time, that pragmatism requires a metaphilosophical "framework" of argumentative premises cast quite strictly in terms of rationalist necessities akin to the necessities of Frege's model; and, alternatively, that Kant himself is best construed in terms of a thoroughly naturalized or pragmatized transcendentalism. I hold instead that the first option is no more than a conceptual masquerade and that the second yields no more than a false Kant.

2.
THE MONGREL FUNCTIONALITY
OF ORDINARY LANGUAGE

I

The very idea of animal forms of encultured learning — especially among the higher mammals, but not restricted to them — often startlingly impressive in spite of being unlanguaged, would make no sense at all if we denied a deeper continuum between animal and human concepts. The idea has an alien ring, I must admit, which (I believe) is only partly due to deep prejudices about animal consciousness, intelligence, thought, and cognition. Recent philosophical fashion — self-characterized as Kantian or, more generally, as rationalist — has tended to marginalize perceptual or allied contributions to the analysis of discursive concepts. I find the economy ill-conceived, deficient when applied to the human infant's impressive mastery of natural languages. Of course, the very idea of a separable concept of any kind is decidedly tenuous. Here, I adopt the irresistible, *en bloc* convenience of supposing that the mental life of the most advanced (languageless) animals fully *justifies* a liberal — albeit heuristically or analogically rendered — use of discursive (enlanguaged) concepts originally and paradigmatically intended to describe and account for the mental life of human persons. Quite frankly: it has proved well-nigh impossible to specify just how an animal's (a dog's, say) putative *use* of a "perceptual concept" (that is, a perceptually grounded, perceptually articulated concept) of a cat differs from a "discursive concept" of a perceived cat, *qua* perceptual concept rather than *discursive* concept-of-a-perceptual-object!

Here, I concede that we model perceptual concepts discursively; but then, we also understand discursive concepts applied to the humanly experienced world as themselves continuous (in some deep way) with the use of perceptual and other nondiscursive concepts. The "liberty" provided may be accounted for in the simplest terms. An animal's actual perceptions of the same structured world we inhabit are effectively read as tantamount to yielding or engaging the enabling "concepts" of such perceptions. That is to say: in viewing the intelligent behavior of a cat (learning, say, to lift the latch of a closet door, in order to explore an interior space) or an ape's shaping a straw-like shoot of grass (in order to collect termites efficiently), we approach as well as possible to the essential Darwinian posit of the continuum of animal and human intelligence. Here, the realist treatment of animal life, species-specific models of rationality, the limited interpretability of animal behavior, the very admission of animal intelligence, the primacy of the precisions of discursive cognition conspire to validate and legitimate the *mongrel* use of the propositionalized resources of linguistic description and explanation. It makes little or no difference here whether we speak of such liberties as fictive, figurative, or heuristic. We have no better options if we are unwilling to deny the intelligence of animals and the fluency of infant learning.

I think it entirely fair to say that, even in our own day, post-Darwin, concepts — the very idea of a concept — have been effectively captured by the Kantian idiom that still dominates our best thought: that is, as being undeniably discursive. But if we concede the intelligence and intelligent behavior of many (unlanguaged) animal species, we may also think, inventively, of concepts as heuristically posited (however discursively modeled) structural abstractions (and idealizations) of the functional components of mental life said to be entailed in obvious manifestations of (animal) intelligence — involving, say, inferential and non-inferential cognition among both enlanguaged and languageless animals: in the case of the latter, perceptually and experientially grounded and operative, without benefit (as yet or ever) of discursive powers. I'm persuaded that discursive and nondiscursive concepts must form an evolutionary continuum and that the human infant's mastery of language makes no sense unless it engages such a continuum. If this is at all reasonable, then the denial of animal concepts, as in familiar Cartesian, Kantian, and Fregean rationalisms, must be a profound mistake. I cannot deny that we approach the analysis of concepts by way of discursive models; but, then, the entire treatment of animal intelligence is heuristically anthropomorphized. I regard this as a particularly important — not unrisky, but distinctly benign — mongrel idiom.

I trust it will have dawned on you that I've laid down at least two essential clues in this and the first lecture regarding the ineliminability of "mongrel" liberties among the fluencies of ordinary discourse: the first, that the artifactual transformation of the human primate into a person requires the admission that the concept of a person begins its own career as a "grammatical fiction" applied to infants learning their first language

— hence, also, to the often-contested standing of the fixity of the self's or person's self-identity — think, here, of the pertinent views of figures like Hume and Derek Parfit and Daniel Dennett; and, second, that we are obliged to describe the nondiscursive concepts of intelligent animals anthropomorphically and anthropocentrically, in discursive ways, even though the practice, construed literally, may be self-contradictory, perhaps even incoherent, certainly contrary in spirit to the thesis that discursive concepts may themselves require animal fluencies involving perceptual concepts in order to be mastered at all. Without pursuing the matter in any depth here, let me suggest that it's impossible to pursue the analysis of "mind" or the "meaning" of ordinary words without an extensive use of mongrel liberties, in order to regularize the effectiveness of quotidian discourse. Hence, a third — an *omnibus* — clue draws on the obvious good sense of acknowledging that the human race could not have postponed its use of the actual languages we use until any or all of them had successfully resolved the philosophical puzzles of how best to construe the right analysis of perfectly commonplace notions! We learn to avoid the traps of using strategically useful terms that we cannot yet satisfactorily define.

I have no idea how the question may be resolved analytically (or at all) wherever we venture detailed structural comparisons between the two sorts of concept. I take the initial heuristic concession to be an admission of the futility of pretending that sustained comparisons of the would-be details of either sort of concept ever overcomes the limitations of the initial liberty of invoking concepts as explanatory at all. Nevertheless, I do indeed believe that many animal species are impressively intelligent and that the initial liberty is not a blunder.

My thought is this: that, for one thing, admitting pertinent Darwinian and post-Darwinian discoveries, we cannot understand the onset and achievement of enlanguaged (or discursive) concepts if we cannot draw on the conceptual powers of unlanguaged human infants — *a fortiori*, on the conceptual powers of ancestral and evolutionarily linked animal species; for another, we cannot understand what we mean, now, by the meaning of words, in a world overwhelmingly accessed in perceptual and experiential ways, unless the perceptual structure of perceivable things can be incorporated or represented in the structure of discursive concepts (which may well be what Aristotle had in mind, in his remarks in the *De Anima*), and unless there is a spontaneously accessible functional similarity between perceptual and discursive concepts; and, third (but hardly last), that the unavoidability of the heuristic strategy itself affords compelling confirmation of the general claim I'm advancing about the ineliminability of the *mongrel* function of ordinary language.[1]

In this way, I bring together the three paradoxes I've set myself the task of exploring in a unified account — regarding persons, language, and the collective nature of enlanguaged societies — and, in examining all that, of making provision for a confrontation between pragmatism and a revived rationalism: one that marks the most salient philosophical *agon* of the moment; casts the Kantian challenge in a particularly arresting form; accommodates the fresh relevance of the so-called Pittsburgh School; facilitates our assessing the prospects of a pragmatism (or near-pragmatism) that openly regards itself as committed to a strong form of rationalism; but then, in turn, finds itself obliged to abandon the primacy of rationalism itself.

The idea, an evolutionary inference, is easily rejected by neo-Cartesians and neo-Kantians, a constraint that, bearing as it does on the disputed rationality and inferential powers of the most advanced animal species, adversely affects our understanding of ourselves as prelinguistic infants (also, then, as mature primates, however transformed into persons). The entire sweep of pre-Darwinian philosophies of mind and epistemology finds itself unsettled by the sparest admissions here: particularly among rationalist "*metaphysics* of cognition" of an exclusionary bent, as distinct from laxer rationalist *methodologies* fitted to the confirmation of selected runs of truth-claims, or distinguished from the pragmatist acceptance of the Darwinian continuum itself. Viewed in the simplest way: if we distinguish between Kant's and Frege's rationalisms, respectively, as metaphysically and methodologically defined, then, by parity of reasoning, the same concession defines (partially at least) the difference between John McDowell's and Robert Brandom's up-to-date rationalisms.[2]

---

1   Here, I must admit to being in awe of Christopher Peacocke's original effort to provide a first model of discursive concepts, in his *A Study of Concepts* (Cambridge: MIT Press, 1992).

2   Compare, for instance, John McDowell, *The Logical Form of an Intuition*, in *Having the World in View: Essays on Kant, Hegel, and Sellars* (Cambridge: Harvard University Press, 2009), pp. 22–43, and Robert B. Brandom, *Categories and Noumena: Two Kantian Axes of Sellars's Thought*, in *From Empiricism to Expressivism: Brandom Reads Sellars* (Cambridge: Harvard University Press, 2015), pp. 30–98, notably p. 31. I press the comparison, because it should be clear that although both the metaphysical and the methodological forms of rationalism tend to deny animal cognition, they do so for very different reasons and with very different consequences. The Cartesian and Kantian maneuvers become completely untenable in the light of the continuum of the animal and the human; the Fregean premise simply has no use for animal cognition (which might be said to be hopelessly psychological).

Which is to say: we've come back to the "Pittsburgh School's" own efforts to test the prospects of reading pragmatism and related analytic movements along decidedly rationalist lines — by reading Sellars, Dewey, and Wittgenstein, chiefly, as naturalized rationalists — whether favoring Kant or Frege or some pertinently shared intention between them, whether transcendental or inferentialist, whether viably or only heuristically foundational. A bold and intriguing conviction, you may say, that I admit I regard as ultimately regressive, entirely unsecured, finally inimical (I should add) to pragmatism's own sense of philosophical rigor and productive innovation. Pragmatism, I say, goes "mongrel" in addressing the quotidian world — verbally as well as philosophically; whereas rationalism insists on the adequate pieties of an elusive and closed rigor that is itself profoundly contested by its own advocates. Here, then, you may glimpse the *agon* of our day, ventured, in good part, in terms of the import of Darwinian and post-Darwinian discoveries about the nature of the human being and (may I add) the reflexive, nearly insuperable difficulties of philosophy itself.

Here, then, we are well advised to distinguish carefully between *modeling* our descriptive and explanatory undertakings and *theorizing* about actual causal mechanisms and the would-be interpretable meanings and significations of mental life. My own intuitions favor, if you can believe it, the marvelously "successful" failure of Mendeleev's fledgling efforts to formulate the table of chemical elements: his hostile rejection of the merest atomism was not enough to deprive him of empirical discoveries of unexpected importance, arrived at by way of an untenable theory and methodology! Clever modeling, it seems, is often better than the false theories that sustain them. Pragmatism is disposed to succor fruitful error by admitting the insuperable presumptions of theorized realism over the instrumental opportunism of sheer modeling. May I suggest that this is as true of Noam Chomsky's computational biology of language as it is of Charles Darwin's market conception of a primitive form of evolutionary genetics?

The decisive lesson here is perfectly straightforward: admitting no more than the inherent difficulty — or effective impossibility — of resolving familiar puzzles of mind, knowledge, meaning, truth and the like, it's clear that the original formation of the conceptual resources of natural languages cannot have been delayed, in order to ensure the adequacy of whatever fledgling philosophical notions may have become linguistically entrenched. Hence, it's a foregone conclusion that, at least with regard to difficult (such) questions, natural languages have always needed (and will always need) to rely on compensatory mongrel devices (both philosophical and nonphilosophical, possibly flagrant) by which apt speakers may finesse or evade inescapably faulty, even absurd, phrasings — or, say, signal, inexplicitly, the need for a special caution or tolerance in ensuring the sincerity and success of chance conversational episodes. I myself tend to read Descartes's dualism as a clear specimen of a "mongrel philosophy" that finds the mind/body puzzle too difficult to resolve — and therefore simply converts philosophical failure into mongrel success. (I read Kant conformably, though at the level of Kant's greater proficiency; I also concede here that that ruling is likely to be strenuously contested.)

On related grounds, I should say, I've never been persuaded by Noam Chomsky's distinctly rationalist (that is, innatist) claims (old style) regarding universal grammar (or, of course, anything like an innatist semantics), largely on the strength of the double intuition that grammatical syntax and semantics are, finally, inseparable, both in logic and linguistics, and that the Chomskyan thesis very nearly eliminates the import of cultural history and, possibly, evolutionary prehistory as well. More recently, however, Chomsky has displayed more than ordinary courage in acknowledging the excessive zeal of his earlier views, in having borrowed (illicitly, it seems, from historical languages) the would-be (modular) invariances of his innatist grammar (UG), without abandoning the rationalist meta-principle on which he has always relied).[3] (That's to say, Chomsky now reads UG as a genetic principle.) But what, in the Chomskyan account, *is* the relevance of the evolutionary continuum of the prehistory of language or the mongrel history of any modern language? I find no clear answer in Chomsky.

II

I concede without quarrel the full benefits of modeling the grammar of natural languages on the observed regularities of cultural use over merely theorizing about the indissoluble unity of the "language organ." Chomsky now treats grammar as a modular description of the brain, along the lines of an essentially neuronal mapping of computable options. Whereas, for what it's worth, I think of the human use of an actual language as an

---

3   See, for instance, Noam Chomsky, *New Horizons in the Study of Language and Mind* (Cambridge: Cambridge University Press, 2000). I offer a closer view of Chomsky's daring concession in my *The Unraveling of Scientism: American Philosophy at the End of the Twentieth Century* (Ithaca: Cornell University Press, 2003), Ch. 1. Of course, speculations of this sort are completely superseded in Chomsky's most recent work.

improvisationally open, culturally and psychologically contexted system of "Intentionally meaningful sound" (or signs), significant or significative, expressive, enabling, serviceable for every purposive interest of persons and societies of persons. Linguistically, grammar and semantic import appear to be inseparable, more nearly reasonably determinable than objectively determinate, collectively possessed and consensually confirmed.

Chomsky regards his own investigations as a form of biology or biolinguistics, almost without a need for human agency; whereas I regard linguistic phenomena primarily in terms of the agentive productions of apt speakers, centered in the processes of "mind" rather than of "brain," even if the mind is ultimately regarded (problematically, I'd say) as the functioning of the brain. In this sense, I subordinate Chomsky's speculations to (for instance) Wittgenstein's intuitions (as in "following a [linguistic] rule") in *Investigations* (but, of course, not merely to Wittgenstein); and I subordinate *both* to the vagaries of the hybrid evolution of human persons, to the effective "metaphysics" of persons and enlanguaged cultures, and to the contingencies of sheer history, experience, and purposive improvisation. On Chomsky's view, "language" tends to be impressively algorithmic; on mine, "language" bluntly exhibits sufficient regularity to be learnable, though whatever regularities appear to be algorithmic or rulelike tend to be constructivist, idealized, and provisional. But then, the "elements" of language itself appear to be decidedly different in the two approaches.

It's not at all clear, for instance, that Chomsky's computationally proposed grammatical algorithms, ingeniously *fitted* to the sub-structures of carefully contrived specimen sentences, actually represent the independently ascribed algorithmic properties of natural-language-discourse itself. This is indeed the *pons* of a linguistics that does not begin with an "empirical" survey of the discernible structure of languages in actual use, but prefers instead to theorize top down from the seemingly remote vantage of a conjectured biology: the impression of an adequate algorithmic idealization may itself be an artifactual illusion (or self-fulfilling "analysis") of Chomsky's Cartesian method. It's entirely possible that Chomsky's "grammatical" uniformities are ingeniously contrived (however sincerely generated), never rightly tested in terms of the normal use of an actual language — though "adequate" for Chomsky's own very different kind of linguistic speculation.

Let me put my primary objection more carefully. I don't deny that there are innate constraints on mental processes (among what we laxly call "thought" or "thinking," as in inference, memory, reference and reidentification, involving both discursive and nondiscursive concepts); and I don't deny that human infants are biologically gifted in ways that enable their remarkably rapid and accurate mastery of *any* of the thousands of natural languages that the human race has produced. But I don't find these (and similar) admissions tantamount to the claim, or strong enough to justify the inference, that language is, essentially or primarily,

> an "organ of the body," more or less on a par with the visual or digestive or immune systems. Like others, it is [Chomsky maintains] a subcomponent of a complex organism that has sufficient internal integrity so that it makes sense to study it in abstraction from its complex interaction with other systems in the life of the organism. In this case it is a cognitive organ, like the systems of planning, interpretation, reflection, and whatever else falls among those aspects of the world loosely "termed mental," which reduce somehow to the "organical structures of the brain," [to speak] in the words of… Joseph Priestley.[4]

I mean, specifically, that though there are essential biological conditions without which human language would be impossible, possibly including — on the strength of Chomsky and Berwick's argument — the computational rule, *Merge*, construed as an innate power of the human brain, read "hierarchically" rather than merely "linearly" (and said to be operative in the human brain but not in that of the chimpanzee or the macaque or song-birds like the Bengalese finch). But, here, I suggest, Berwick and Chomsky's theory obliquely supports my own theory, though *their* literal affirmations plainly do not! Berwick, for example, advances the strong (entirely convincing) claim: "Most human language syntactic properties are not found in birdsong. The only exceptions relate to the properties of human language systems."[5] Of course. *If* "sound systems" are not, as such, language systems, or if "vocal properties" manifest a linguistically relevant role only when they are actually used *in* "human language sound systems" then it's not unreasonable (however remarkable it may be) that "birdsong is only a model for speech," if it is that, or, better, if it is only a model for making the use of language aurally accessible as speech. That's to

---

4   Robert C. Berwick and Noam Chomsky, *Why Only Us: Language and Evolution* (Cambridge: MIT Press, 2016), p. 56. I add, parenthetically, that this latest book, jointly authored with Robert Berwick, is an impressively strong defense of the thesis informally defined above, as well as of a good many other of Chomsky's detailed claims. (This is Chomsky at his best.) Nevertheless, I'm persuaded that a fruitful dispute (with Chomsky) would confirm that some of his claims draw on a deep equivocation on the use of the term "language" in speaking of human languages. Chomsky's formulation may be even more extreme in Noam Chomsky, *What Kind of Creature Are We?* (New York: Columbia University Press, 2016), Ch. 1.

5   Berwick and Chomsky, *Why Only Us*, p. 140.

say, it's hardly unreasonable (though it is *largely* irrelevant) to conjecture (where we must conjecture) that there happen to be "syllabic" and "lettrist" analogies between birdsong and human speech — often startling, as with ravens and parrots.

Now, I think the same is true (and for much the same reason) with *Merge* itself (Chomsky's computational rule). Chomsky and Berwick maintain:

> Every computational system has embedded within it somewhere an operation that applies to two objects X and Y already formed, and constructs from them a new object Z. Call this operation Merge. SMT [the Strong Minimalist Thesis: that is, the thesis "that the generative process is optimal... keeps to the simplest recursive operation designed to satisfy interface conditions in accord with independent principles of efficient computation"] dictates that Merge will be as simple as possible: it will not modify X or Y or impose an arrangement on them; in particular, it will leave them unordered.... Merge is therefore just set formation: Merge of X and Y yields the set {X, Y}.[6]

I see no pointedly linguistic thesis here regarding actual human languages; I do see a ground-level constraint that appears (as Chomsky says) in "every computational system," for instance in pertinent biological systems, without reference to language at all. Merge, however, is meant to be a higher-order principle (in linguistic analysis) that permits the conjunction just mentioned to generate an infinitely iterative, hierarchically defined array of new objects of the sort mentioned; and *that* systematic feature turns out to serve Chomsky's theory very well, despite not being confirmed from the perspective of the empirical analysis of languages in actual use. (Where something like "Merge" obtains in the analysis of an actual language, it will be applied to "words" and not to "word-like" entities that never appear in actual languages.) But this is not an inherently linguistic matter; it's only because it's human languages — *not* Nim's (the well-known chimpanzee's) and not the Bengalese finches' failure to master "nonlinear or hierarchical patterns" — that count: it's only that true language *is*, in the pertinent respect, itself hierarchically structured (according to Chomsky's thesis).

Chomsky does not explore the putative feats of the bonobo Kanzi. He makes one problematic remark about the inaccessibility of the Kanzi studies (p. 177); but they appear to challenge the scope of his own generalizations when read in terms of the theory of language he does *not* favor (where,

---

6   Berwick and Chomsky, *Why Only Us*, p. 98; the explanation of "SMT" appears at
     p. 71.

for instance, his algorithmic claims may be less than compelling, even with regard to apt speakers of natural languages). Nor does he consider the possibility that Neanderthal or Denisovan man *might*, though he lacked (if indeed he lacked) the determinative proteins thought to make hierarchical language-like processing accessible, have produced a linearly-ordered language-like instrument closer to the limitations of the chimpanzees. We are unable (at present) to say anything confirmable about such possibilities. But can it be ruled out as biologically impossible? Steven Pinker, I should add, seems to think that human infants, in their first attempts at learning an adult language, often favor linear snippets of language (as, apparently, chimpanzees do as well — for different reasons).[7] Why not? But, then, Pinker favors "language learnability" in the psychological rather than in any merely computational sense. There's the point of the counter-argument.

There's no doubt that Chomsky has made hugely important contributions in demonstrating that language is profoundly dependent on biological resources. But I don't believe he's shown that language (in the narrow sense of specifically natural languages) *is* suitably explained in biological terms. Chomsky avoids the psychological, the cultural, the historical, the interpretive, the nonalgorithmic as much as possible. We're back to the innovations of thought made possible by the cultural transformation of primates into persons. I cannot spare space enough for this important matter. But let me simply mention two further admissions (from Chomsky) that strengthen the drift of my objection: first, regarding "words," the vocabulary or lexicon to which grammars (or rules of order) are applied:

> The atomic elements [of a language: ideally, an "I-language," in Chomsky's idiom] pose deep mysteries. The minimal meaning-bearing elements of human languages — wordlike, but not words — are radically different from anything known in animal communication systems. Their origin is entirely obscure, posing a very serious problem for the evolution of human cognitive capacities, language in particular... Careful examination shows that widely held doctrines about the nature of these elements are untenable: crucially, the widely held referentialist doctrine that words pick out extramental objects.[8]

You realize that these "wordlike [elements], but not words" *are* the as yet unformulizable "elements" of Chomsky's theory of language! Hence, the passage just cited must be joined to a second, to permit us to gain a

---

7   See Steven Pinker, *Language Learnability and Language Development* (Cambridge: Harvard University Press, 1984).
8   Berwick and Chomsky, *Why Only Us*, pp. 90–91.

proper sense of the state of Chomsky's inclusive theory. That's to say, we are to think of "language as a biological object, internal to an individual, and capturing what we may call the Basic Property of human language," namely: that

> each language yields a digitally infinite array of hierarchically structured expressions with systematic interpretations at interfaces with two other internal systems, the sensorimotor system for externalization and the conceptual system for inference, interpretation, planning, organization of action, and other elements of what is informally called "thought".[9]

I regard this as a reasonable proposal: that's to say, *within* the terms of a "Cartesian science" of language. Chomsky labels such a language an "internal or I-language"; its theory "is Universal Grammar (UG) [the nomological or algorithmic regularities of grammar]... the theory of the genetic component of the faculty of language, the capacity that makes it possible to acquire and to use particular I-languages".[10]

What's seriously missing is the systematic or theoretical relationship between the description of words and sentences of actual human languages and the postulated "elements" of computable I-languages open to explanation under UG (now genetically construed) — so that every "historical" language could, in principle, be mapped in terms of its vocabulary and grammar read approximatively in terms of one or another I-language (in computationally rendered genetic terms). But the instruments provided for the characterization of an I-language do not (*yet*) apply "theoretically" to the parsing of languages or explaining the structure of actual languages *qua* languages in actual use! We would have to be able to show that I-languages *are* genetically and computationally robust possibilities for explaining the structure of actual languages, where independent analyses of actual languages addressed to the salient features of usage (bearing on interpretable meaning, syntax, forms of thinking, contexts of use, and the like) *confirm* the plausibility of invoking the "organ" model itself.

The trick is that the validity of Chomsky's biological theory *depends* on fitting the analysis of actual languages to his model, without undue circularity. I find the "circularity" benign enough. But I cannot see the force of the entire argument if it lacks an account of the treatment of meaning and thought *in user-specific terms*. In fact, I cannot make satisfactory sense of Chomsky's thesis that "language is well designed for computational

---

9   Berwick and Chomsky, *Why Only Us*, 89–90.
10   Berwick and Chomsky, *Why Only Us*, p. 90.

efficiency and expression of thought, but poses problems for use, in particular for communication; ...language [Chomsky holds] is, in essence, an instrument of thought...".[11] That thesis is well-nigh tautological if we're speaking of I-languages; and, apart from some overlap in purpose, very nearly dead wrong if we're speaking of actual languages. If, for instance, one takes Wittgenstein's argument against private languages seriously, then the *conditions* of discursive thought itself ineluctably presuppose the collective or communal sharing of an actual language. I don't deny the complexity of the communicative problem — but then I take that to be a more fundamental question regarding the syntactic and semantic properties of actual languages than Chomsky apparently does! That's to say, the abstract question of its admission begins to explain the fundamental difference between what may be called a "Cartesian linguistics" addressed to evolutionary survival and an "actualist" linguistics (my own coinage) addressed to successful conversation and the like.

I've taken more than a permissible run of space and time to address Chomsky's important thesis, because, of course, it's obvious that my own theory, which I take to be reconcilable (at least in part) with Chomsky's very bold claims, goes completely contrary to the purpose of Chomsky's argument. *I* want to know what a word is; what it is to understand the meaning of what we actually say; what sort of uncertainty is communicatively tolerable in ordinary discourse (and how and why); and what devices have we for managing misunderstanding, misinterpretation, creative uses of language, and related puzzles (which Chomsky himself acknowledges).[12]

I'll add a very brief final aside. Painting, in the sense practiced in the Western world — let us say, from Manet to roughly the end of Picasso's life — manifests stylistic and semiotic properties somewhat analogous to the applicability of grammar and linguistic meaning to the operative "atoms" of language — words, in natural languages. Moreover, painting itself presupposes the mastery of language, as well as a grasp of the enlanguaged, publicly accessible world that painting addresses, expresses, represents, interprets, and responds to — by way of visual images. Painting generates what appear to be complex nonlinear structures of its own. I have no doubt that, for numerous "movements" within the career of Western painting — early Cubism, for instance, or classic de Stijl — debatable regularities can be made out that might well tempt us to think of painting

---

11   Berwick and Chomsky, *Why Only Us*, p. 107.
12   See, especially, Chomsky, *What Kind of Creature Are We?*, pp. 14–16. Here, Chomsky flatly asserts: "there is no need for meanings to be shared (or sounds, or structures)" (p. 15). Imagine!

in quasi-algorithmic ways, even if we suppose the literal notion to be preposterous. Here, imputed structures appear to be *ad hoc* models keyed to understanding particular works, themselves informed by attending to what might reasonably be supposed to have been "uttered" (intended, in some generous sense, that need not require evidentiary avowals from the artists said to have produced them). I'm aware that Chomsky explicitly says, in *Why Only Us*:

> it's not our purpose here to write a book on natural language processing. Our point is simply that there are *many* different types of algorithms to explore, each with different possible implications for both psychologistic fidelity and evolutionary change — if one imagines that efficient parsing somehow matters for evolutionary success.[13]

Chomsky and Berwick mention specimens, here, involving "serial computation" that appear to belong to actual language use; similar results can be expected, they say, from "parallel algorithms for Merge-type language parsing."[14] I don't doubt for a moment that that's true. But the objective of all these maneuvers surely includes (cannot fail to include) facilitating our understanding *what is actually said* — or uttered in the way of a painting. That's to say: in existential contexts, in life itself, within our form of life. Don't our heroes need *some* account of "natural language processing" to justify *their* applying *algorithmic modeling* to the confirmation of a *theory of natural language* suited to the valid parsing and interpretation of the yield of such languages? Painting, I concede, especially in our time, tends to avoid the routines of easy legibility: in fact, we positively prize its more difficult interpretive conundrums. But we never fail to work at resolving them; and we believe that we can succeed and that understanding painting requires such an effort, *and* that we bring our theories of painting into accord with whatever that requires. Now, does Chomsky think there are or there are not plausible runs of spontaneous discourse — involving slang, shorthand efficiencies, conceptual uncertainties, second-language bafflements, poetic intricacies, vaguenesses, ambiguities, polysemous vocabularies, obliquely embedded quotations, improvisations instantly required (and so understood), errors passingly flagged (often not corrected), awkwardnesses of every kind — that infect the general use of language all the time, that cannot be explicated by computational or algorithmic strategies alone or primarily or at all?

---

13 Berwick and Chomsky, *Why Only Us?*, p. 138.
14 Berwick and Chomsky, *Why Only Us?*, p. 138.

III

I may then now add — to Chomsky's brave but (to my mind) unconvincing dictum about universal grammars — a further word about other problematic speculations regarding natural-language use that have, similarly, acquired a dubious eminence in our time. Here I include, especially, Wittgenstein's excessive confidence in the import of the functional adequacy of ordinary language, shrewdly championed in *Philosophical Investigations*, obliquely directed against the rational formalism advanced by Gottlob Frege and favored (in a very different way) by Bertrand Russell, now made fashionable through the following phrasing of Wittgenstein's quietism (also known as his "philosophical therapy"), possibly, then, a counter-rationalism of Wittgenstein's own invention:

> Philosophy [Wittgenstein affirms] may in no way interfere with the actual use of language; it can in the end only describe it. For it cannot give it any foundation either. It leaves everything as it is. It also leaves mathematics as it is, and no mathematical discovery can advance it.[15]

There's philosophical overkill for you! I deem Wittgenstein to have been arbitrary here, possibly (also) vindictive against the rationalists (Frege, for instance). But to readmit philosophy's pertinence in "correcting" both ordinary usage *and* philosophical *dicta* — bear in mind the comic ambiguity of Wittgenstein's own pronouncement (*Investigations*, §255): "The philosopher's treatment of a question [whether about mathematical facts or about the right use of ordinary language] is like the treatment of an illness" — you realize that my remarks about Chomsky's treatment of linguistics were an unavoidable but sizeable aside. I suppose we may fairly claim that philosophy and philosophical therapy are, intentionally, more or less inseparable: hence, that the definition of pragmatism's own "corrections" (viewed in terms of language: mongrel language in particular) lies somewhere between Chomsky's and Wittgenstein's excesses, with the ineluctable proviso that, dialectically, Chomsky and Frege remain entitled to their own rationalist rejoinders — and *we* may wish to find an ampler form of reunification.

Wittgenstein's words are perhaps no more than an expression of annoyance, hardly a defensible thesis, in the light of any post-Darwinian account of persons and natural language — *and* his own practice. But

---

15   Ludwig Wittgenstein, *Philosophical Investigations*, trans. G.E.M. Anscombe (New York: Macmillan, 1953), Pt. I, §124.

beyond all that, the needs and uses and fashions of ordinary language change continually and must be monitored as best we can. Think here, for instance, of the intransigent (almost unbelievably successful) dualism of our idiom regarding mind and body (hardly altered since Descartes's time), which we continue to employ as an efficient instrument for evading the constant threat of intolerable conceptual defeat (should we attempt to replace our apparent ontology of mind!) in contexts that oblige us to hurry on to more pressing matters that hardly object to our use of carefully fashioned faulty doctrines which, of course, apt speakers fully comprehend. It has its mongrel role to play, but it nevertheless puts discursive fluency at inescapable risk. We tend to ensure discursive efficiency by simplifying (as far as possible) the messages we are obliged to share with others: in conversation, we sometimes reduce them (if we must) to negligible social noise. Wittgenstein does not dwell on the ubiquity of these considerations. But they rightly challenge his philosophical advice.

Add now to the mix, Frege's would-be *exposé* of the structural defects of natural languages, viewed from the vantage of a corrective *application* of the *Begriffsschrift* model (*Begriffsschrift* "thoughts") to the very different medium of ordinary language.[16] I surmise that once the admirable rigor of the *Begriffsschrift* was separated from Frege's logicist objective (in effect, its all but exclusive commitment to arithmetic), the temptation to construct a potentially inclusive rationalist "metaphilosophical framework" for the unity of science (and a feasible extension to the entire sweep of ordinary language use) proved irresistible to a great many philosophical conjectures. I don't, however, find any actual argument in either Brandom or Sellars strong enough to confirm the promise of such enabling boundary conditions among the natural sciences or pragmatic contexts of discourse thought to resemble, sufficiently, Frege's picture of the structure of arithmetical reasoning. The perceptual and intentional entanglements of empirically grounded sciences seem much too strong (and too closely associated with realist arguments) to yield to the alien primacy of numbers.

You sense, therefore, the somewhat guarded admiration for Frege's achievement, in informed pronouncements like the following, advanced by Danielle Macbeth:

---

16   For a sketch of Frege's proposal, see Macbeth, *Realizing Reason*, Ch. 7. See, also, Gottlob Frege, *Begriffsschrift, a formula language, modeled upon that of arithmetic, for pure thought*, (1879), in *Frege and Gödel: Two Fundamental Texts in Mathematical Logic*, ed. Jean van Heijenoort (Cambridge: Harvard University Press, 1970), pp. 1–82.

On Frege's account as here developed [Macbeth claims], it is only through thoughts [Fregean "thoughts"] expressed by sentences in a sufficiently advanced scientific language that one perceives (more generally, has cognitive access to) anything at all. All our knowledge is essentially mediated by an inherently historical, learned public language.[17]

You see the apparent double jeopardy: nothing, Macbeth affirms, can be known "*at all*," except within the terms of a suitable rationalist "framework" (perhaps *this* is the final meaning of Sellars's well-worn phrase, "the space of reasons," viewed from a jointly Kantian and Fregean vantage); *and*, then, what we learn in this way is itself always mediated, perilously, by a contingent and changeable "public language" (effectively, a mongrel language) that has an entirely different agenda to fulfill. The first condition I deem to be an honest wish; the second, a fateful fact the first is meant to override.

Macbeth offers her reading as effectively seconding Frege's reading of his own project. But then, *we lack* "a sufficiently advanced scientific language" by means of which we might claim to discern some suitably enabling Fregean "thoughts" capable of confirming *that* our knowledge of the world does indeed depend on a prior rationalist framework or methodology akin (at least minimally) to that of the *Begriffsschrift*. Perhaps we can never rule out the Fregean option; but Brandom's efforts along these lines fail to convince me that the rationalist model can serve productively enough in its would-be "regulative" role. It seems to function more in the way of one of Max Weber's "ideal type" constructions. Which, cast in the coarsest way, answers to empiricist rather than rationalist intuitions. I suggest that ordinary discourse always protects its mongrel functionality among its usual services, and that pragmatism is its self-appointed philosophical champion.

I read Wittgenstein's remarks more as an indirect warning against Frege and Russell than as an explicit ruling in favor of a strong disjunction between the incompletely systematizable "descriptions" of the regularities of ordinary discourse and any systematization of the language of mathematical reasoning (conceived as a paradigm of "pure thought," in Frege's sense, whatever that may prove to be). It's the same Wittgenstein who clarifies his philosophical therapy this way:

---

17   Danielle Macbeth, *Frege's Logic* (Cambridge: Harvard University Press, 2005), p. 153.

> It [is] true to say that our considerations could not be scientific ones...
> And we may not advance any kind of theory. There must not be anything
> hypothetical in our considerations. We must do away with *explanation*, and
> description alone must take its place, and this description gets its light, that is
> to say, its purpose — from the philosophical problems. These are, of course,
> not empirical problems; they are solved, rather, by looking into the workings of
> our language, and that in such a way as to make us recognize those workings: *in
> spite of* an urge to misunderstand them. The problems are solved, not by giving
> new information, but by arranging what we have always known. *Philosophy*
> is a battle against the bewitchment of our intelligence by means of language.[18]

But, of course, "bewitchment" lurks wherever one finds it — possibly,
then, *in* ordinary discourse as in philosophy: especially if we admit mongrel
liberties; and then, it may be open to therapeutic relief by specifically
philosophical means!

What Wittgenstein says here is not meant to be apodictic (in anything
like the Fregean or Cartesian way); yet it remains stubbornly, inexplicably
assured, in the seemingly fair sense in which the apt speakers of a natural
language have been effectively immersed in an enculturing discipline,
though they may not be able to explain their linguistic fluency, except
circularly — in terms of an original baptism in their home language.
Philosophy, not unlike a first language, is at times a motley lacking any
discernible foundations or any complete set of rules; or, as in the analysis
of mind, meaning, knowledge, truth, and the like, it may simply be unable
to escape circular explanation or unable to parse its own puzzles in a
fresh way. Ordinary discourse is often completely formulaic, inflexible,
uninstructive, even vacuous and misguided in its apparent claims. But even
such defects may mark the promised advantage of its mongrel function. In
fact, such obvious defects, sustained over time, are, generally, favorably
regarded mongrel liberties. (Consider Cartesian dualism again!)

Isn't this precisely what is missing in Chomsky's conception of
language? It's not biology that "enlanguages" successive cohorts of
infants: it's *Bildung*, cultural immersion in an already artifactualized
world peopled by apt speakers of the languages in question, who are
themselves the artifactual transforms of prior suitably "immersed"
primates. As far as I know, Chomsky does not venture a theory of
the origination of true language (that is, natural language). He does
advance the thought that language is a "mental organ," an organ for
"thought," *not* primarily intended for "communication." But discursive

---

18   Wittgenstein, *Philosophical Investigations*, Pt. I, §109.

thought cannot be solipsistic and cannot be mastered without some form of *Bildung*. And that means that private thought and public communication are inseparable. I'm entirely willing to admit that the advent of language may have been a supreme evolutionary sport — that simply happened to succeed in the wildest way. In any case, language's "communicative" function cannot be captured by the impoverished idea of "externalization." Communication signifies the public sharing of the entire bounty of thought and remembered culture. Externalization (in Chomsky's sense) may well be "secondary," but "communication" must be fundamental, and must affect (in important ways) the structure of human language itself.[19]

---

19   Here, surely, Chomsky is mistaken. He says: "language evolved for thought and interpretation: it is fundamentally a system of meaning... Externalization at the sensorimotor level, then, is an ancillary process, reflecting properties of the sensory modality used, with different arrangements, for speech and sign. It would also follow that the modern doctrine that communication is somehow the 'function' of language is mistaken," *Why Only Us*, p. 101. But economies of computationality are not economies of genetics; and efficiencies of human biological evolution are not efficiencies of the evolution of enlanguaged culture. There's a *non sequitur* in leaping from externalization to communication! On Chomsky's own view, the first may be confined to the linear, whereas the second may (on linguistic grounds) be hierarchical.

This leads directly to a deeper mistake on Chomsky's part: "what... has evolved [Chomsky affirms] is, of course, not languages but rather the capacity for language — that is, UG. Languages change, but they do not evolve" (pp. 90–92). Of course, the "capacity for language" evolves biologically — by *Merge* (*if* Chomsky is right in his conjecture); but *language* also "evolves," *not* (or not ordinarily by biological means) but, more correctly, by means of cultural transmission and related processes: for instance, in the abandonment of Latinate inflections among most (but not all) of the Romance languages, and (perhaps) in the case (as has been explained to me) that Czech came to displace, in some episodic and irregular way, its original Slavic grammar, by means of substitutions from a Germanic grammar, which must have affected (as a result of its involvement with the Austro-Hungarian empire) the semantic features of the original language. Of course, history *is* cultural evolution. But if it is, then we have good reason to believe that the evolution of language cannot be expected to be neatly computational. I cannot see how Chomsky can give us assurances on that score.

Chomsky also affirms that "All human languages draw from a fixed, finite inventory, a basic set of articulatory gestures, such as whether to vibrate vocal cords... In short, [he continues] what 'menu changes' languages opt for can vary, but what's on the menu does not" (p. 55). I don't see how this squares with Chomsky's thesis that language itself probably arose, evolutionarily, from a small rewiring of the brain. If so, then why couldn't it happen again in some completely unanticipated way? Certainly, if post-Darwinian evolution will have to accommodate technological intervention (as indeed it already has, in the very

All this may indeed provide the key to part of what is meant, nowadays, in speaking of Wittgenstein's "quietism": that is, his implied retreat to the passing reliabilities (such as they are) of one or another incipient form of *Bildung*, in the face of the potential derailments of excessive philosophical zeal — possibly, for instance, against new-fangled forms of pragmatism. Of course, "Wittgensteinians" take the master at his word — and, thus, Wittgenstein himself often fails us in a way that has been overlooked by his champions and detractors alike. Here, I draw your attention to his failure to consider the immensely important mongrel function of ordinary language — ignored as well, for Fregean-like reasons, by Brandom. (There's one *pons* at least against Brandom's inferentialism.) For, if the mongrel thesis is conceded, I should have to add that Brandom's inferentialism would be seen at once to be impossible to defend: I mean, the executive doctrine that holds that pragmatism must go "analytic" in the Fregean way if it is ever to defend its classic intuition. According to Brandom, it must embrace the primacy of "material inference" (Sellars's term) over noninferential observation (John Dewey's and William James's putatively misbegotten concessions to the "Myth of the Given") — a completely false finding, if ever I saw one — certainly nowhere secured.

On the supposed argument, philosophy must admit the "regulative," heuristic, Fregean-like "metaphilosophical framework" of rationalist argumentation, if it may reasonably claim any epistemological rigor at all. This is my reading (you may remember) of Macbeth's dictum as well. There you may espy the new steel of rationalism's revival, intended to retrieve the best of Kant, Frege, Carnap, Sellars, Wittgenstein, and the Pittsburghers — sometimes, if needed, turned against the backsliding of its own champions.[20]

Let's be clear. Language — that's to say, the least reliance on ordinary language: Wittgenstein's warning, perhaps, that philosophy (read here, Fregean rationalism) — cannot justify its unwelcome analysis of the conditions of any inferentialist structure said to be embedded in the seemingly informal resources of speech. It is itself undermined by Brandom's ingenuities in returning a wayward Fregean (Wittgenstein himself) to the rationalist flock: this time, by a heuristic argument, not

---

advent of language), then there is no basis for insisting on a "fixed, finite inventory" of any kind.

20 See Richard Rorty, *Dewey between Hegel and Darwin*, in *Truth and Progress* (*Philosophical Papers*, vol. 3) (Cambridge: Cambridge University Press, 1998), pp. 290–306; and Robert B. Brandom, *Articulating Reasons: An Introduction to Inferentialism* (Cambridge: Harvard University Press, 2000), *Introduction*.

a constitutively "regulative" maneuver of the *Begriffsschrift* sort! (That is the upshot of "placing" inferentialism within the *lebensformlich* boundaries of ordinary discourse.) The Frege of the *Begriffsscrift* cannot defeat the Wittgenstein of the *Investigations*. The rationalist revival is distinctly arbitrary, undefended, seriously challenged by Brandom himself, irreconcilably opposed to Brandom's admission that pragmatic contexts of material inference are "massively nonmonotonic".[21] "Metaphilosophical" necessities are, as a consequence, dead in the water. If you see the force of the objection, you see as well the fresh import of the mongrel function of ordinary discourse: it reveals Wittgenstein's pragmatist affinities.

Still, you would be completely justified to dwell on the irony that Wittgenstein, deceived (as he believed he was) by Russell's Fregean — at least partially Fregean — conviction, interposes his own seemingly autonomous discipline between an empirically-minded science and philosophy and ordinary discourse about the world we occupy, namely, "therapeutic philosophy" meant to preserve or restore ordinary language's putative sufficiency, free of superfluous philosophical intrusions, but not, it seems, adequately protected against the unnoticed risks of defective, possibly unmarked, possibly ungrounded, possibly benign or tolerable (though faulty) theorizing: proto-Cartesian, for instance, where conceptual imagination fails us — or where we cannot wait long enough for an adequate new solution. The simple counterargument to Wittgenstein's confidence, I suggest, would explain the sense in which the ordinary conversational functions of a natural language cannot be abandoned and cannot be completely replaced (or shored up) by any putatively better language or replaced in one holist gulp by the invention of another language possessing an entirely different structure.

Nothing but a natural language (with all its puzzling features), which persists in its own history (though we can always imagine a "better language" than the one we speak!) could possibly service what I have called language's *mongrel* function — prepared to accommodate the needs of any and every viable function of language, though not itself primarily committed to the bare accuracy or validity or objective fit between its apparent categories and the "true nature" of the real world (whatever that

---

21   See Brandom, *From Empiricism to Expressivism*, Ch. 5. The phrase "massively nonmonotonic" appears at p. 192, which Brandom softens along heuristic lines at p. 194. I have no objection to the "heuristic" use of the model, but I cannot see how it can be elevated to its apparent "primacy" over the intuitions of the classic pragmatists. Brandom offers his own pretty ideology here, but I don't find the convincing argument that he requires.

may be taken to be). For the moment, I'm content to claim no more than that *if* that's true, then the Fregean and Wittgensteinian options may be viewed as opposed distortions of language's mongrel function: which, to be sure, is "idealized," "constructed," "fictionalized" in all the diversely contrived senses in which it is itself used as a viable and sufficiently reliable idiom, apt (say) for confirming truth-claims addressed to the commonsense quotidian world. Generally, mongrel discourse is meant to be "as good as we need" for the practical occasion that confronts us. Mongrel conventions, somehow consensually supported, that trade (at least occasionally) on ultimately indefensible claims, read literally — Cartesian dualism, most compellingly — may be as useful as any that we may devise.

There's the paradoxical clue to the puzzles of this second lecture. The mongrel function of natural language positively thrives on deliberate vagueness, indeterminacy, equivocation, *ad hoc* improvisation, error, ignorance, inconsistency, empty placeholders, opposed and uncertain purposes, passing fictions that masquerade as substances of some familiar quotidian sort that need hardly be challenged or confirmed in all their presumed adequacy. It relies on a shared, decidedly lax sense of the tolerable sufficiency of language that collectively vouchsafes the verbal proprieties of all the utterances of its risked but loyal speakers. I have in mind all that we "take for granted" addressed to the fickle constancies of an inconstant "common" or "commonsense" world, itself a contrived, abstracted, idealized, often deformed, insufficiently trustworthy, partly fictionalized "reality," that we are persuaded accords *"well enough for our own needs"* with our sense of the underlying reality of the experienced world — however that may be finally described.

On the whole, we take language to be an orderly and effectively reliable instrument addressed to an orderly and reliable world, deemed "real" or "actual" in an indefinitely extended nonce fashion, insofar as we succeed, tolerably well (by our own lights), in continually completing our practical ventures — or in claiming to understand why we've failed in some particular undertaking. We assure ourselves in a patently circular way, though sensibly enough, somewhat *aware* of what we admit to be the risks and defects of our inescapable form of life. Neither Frege nor Wittgenstein concedes the adventitious conditions on which their own strictures depend. I take the correction and the method of correction to define pragmatism's abiding lesson for our time. In a word, the Fregean variant of the Pittsburghers' rationalism — never more than arbitrarily invoked — is assuredly toxic to the more modest sufficiencies of classic pragmatism. I mean quite simply: the would-be rigors of the neo-Fregeans are never more than regressive when displaced from arithmetic to the actual world we inhabit. (Wishes can't be horses.)

We share a language — or we share the mongrel functionality of a home language — that enables aggregated humans to sustain a viable sense of a social and humanly familiar world (*a fortiori*, a shared material world), local and global at the same time, the perceived constancy of which actually *depends* on our accommodating its contrived resources, its serviceable distortions and liberties, its adventurous but hardly demonstrable economies. It's the serviceability of ordinary language that is its most important feature. (I return to this neglected theme in my third lecture.) It arises as an immense improvement over the power and range of prelinguistic communication; and its apparent adequacy must originally have been sensed in terms somewhere (in the early phases of the continuum) between maturing primates and incipient persons. But the decisive fact that guides the history of any natural language lies with the inherent difficulty of philosophical puzzles themselves — those especially that have to do with the formation and function of persons and their enlanguaged world: meaning, knowledge, truth, mind, thought, judgment, validity, mutual understanding, and the like. These matters are nearly as difficult to plumb at the present time as they must have been when primate humans first became reflective. There's the source of the muddled plausibility of claims in favor of the mongrel function of ordinary language. The verbal solution of the specimen puzzles I've mentioned may, conceivably, always require some mongrel tricks to function at all.

We typically work with a loosely contrived conception of a viable world — the shadow of our actual world (Plato's Cave, perhaps) — a "mid-world" as I sometimes call it, that answers to our mongrel competences: part realist, part fictional, prudently approximative, open to being suitably discounted in an entirely literal-minded way, best suited to customary interests that have themselves become habitual, subject always to whatever degrees of precision our competences are able to capture. Mongrel discourse, then, is fitted to the ordinary, the typical, the existential, the already familiar, the imperfectly (but pertinently) understood — in effect, the consensual — in that extraordinary sense in which any random aggregate of speakers of the same language readily discerns the mongrel idiom that serves its members "well enough" for the nonce occasion that includes them (without explicit or continual reorientation). I view this as a sympathetic reckoning of what Dewey may well have had in mind (in part at least) in his well-known characterizations of a "problematic" or "indeterminate situation."[22] (He

---

22   See John Dewey, *Logic: The Theory of Inquiry* (New York: Henry Holt, 1938).

saw the need for mongrel provisions in contexts of agentive uncertainty.) In this sense, epistemology and metaphysics function best in informal ways. They need not aim at ultimate truth; they may be merely "warranted" by the occasion. There is no uniquely correct characterization of what is real: the real is whatever answers to mundane life, and its description includes at least whatever issues from mongrel discourse.

The precision of the sciences themselves depends on the laxities and liberties of ordinary discourse and is undoubtedly qualified by that fact: in the sense, both, that the conceptual limitations of the material world are restrictions posited within the amplitude of the agentive life of persons and in the sense that precision is itself a graded norm defined within the competence of a mongrel language. I see in this, I should add, the inversion of the unity-of-science conception: every science is a human science, and the physical sciences require a restriction and simplification of the vocabulary and explanatory options of the human sciences. Wholesale reduction — or mongrel replacement — in the opposite direction is impossible, which, I believe, Sellars grudgingly came to realize and accept: the growing challenge to his scientism.

IV

Let me offer a small illustration of what I have been claiming. I say we literally become the persons we are — we transform ourselves spontaneously, primate into person, at first inchoately — when, in the very process of mastering language, we begin to experience ourselves, discursively (as by avowal), as the proprietary site of experiencing whatever comes to count as what we rightly thus avow or express (in sensibility, thought, memory, speech and behavioral responses to what we experience).

We learn to experience reflexively — we experience our perceiving what we perceive, for instance — what, in discursive terms, typically yields what we call "awareness" or "self-consciousness" or (even) "consciousness of self." But these formulations are already seriously equivocal, stubbornly difficult to displace in reductive ways, centered instrumentally and incommensurably in terms of existential interests, resistant to mathematized, algorithmic, nomological, monotonic regularities: awareness of self and reflexive awareness in sensory experience are not at all the same thing. Even uncomprehendingly, as prelinguistic infants, we begin, by rote, to produce the existential thickness of our embodied perceptual and experiential awareness of what, with the developing mastery of language, will standardly come to count as the content of our inner mental life as persons. In learning a language, we begin with a fictively contrived grammatical identity, which we hardly understand initially but which we automatically transform, by iterated reflexive reference, into a palpable agentive and expressive self — the decisive *pons* of classic "unity of science." (Just sample the self-deceptive scientisms of Sellars and Carl Hempel.)

A fair case can be made, to the effect that awareness (in this transformative sense) requires an adequate mastery of language: a palpable sense of the evolving presence of an experiencing self capable of indefinitely extended reflexive and Intentional functions — responding purposively (say) to the experience of a signal (a traffic light's turning red, for instance). But it needs to be said as well that, among the higher animals at least, any reasonably normal *sensory* experience is already regularly, inherently, non-relationally qualified by some sort of creaturely reflexive ("self-aware") experience, despite being unlanguaged and inseparable from mere sensibility itself. It cannot, of course, be taken to signify the incipience or presence of an actual person; nevertheless, sensibility in a living organism comes to be seen as manifesting an inherent reflexivity more primitive than any agentive impulse.[23]

Think, for instance, of a house cat's being aware that, in being stroked affectionately, its body is being touched. (The description, I concede, cannot but be anthropomorphized — very probably, then, misleadingly.) Nevertheless, there is some reflexive, unbidden centeredness in the perceptions and experiences of the higher animals that, in a way, anticipates the discursive transform that, functionally, we call a self — or at least an incipience in the direction of apperceptive integrity below any level of discursivity. (Kant would never allow any such admission: it would have undermined the first *Critique*.) I take the acknowledgement to support the idea of a continuum of animal (*perceptual*, experiential, behavioral) concepts and person-level (*discursive*) concepts. It's well-nigh impossible to master language if one lacks the sensory and experiential resources that infants must apply in acquiring their first language, drawing on their prelinguistic abilities to discern the perceptible structures of perceived things, apparently assimilable within perceptually formed and perceptually

---

23 I believe Kant was dawningly aware of the inevitable sham of having assigned freedom to the noumenal world; and I read Ernst Cassirer's final account of the "cultural sciences" as a stylish segue to the inevitably post-rationalist reckoning of Kant's (and his own) "regularism." See Ernst Cassirer, *The Logic of the Cultural Sciences*, trans. S. G. Lofts (New Haven: Yale University Press, 2000), Study 3.

operative concepts.[24] This alone suggests the sense in which Kant overstates the role of language in the lowest forms of apperception or their analogues in sensibility. Kant's account (in the first *Critique*) is uncharacteristically incautious. (We must remember that Kant is attempting to present his new form of rationalism, free of any taint of the cognate doctrines of his own day that he's actually combating.)

I now add — out of the blue — that there's no compelling reason to suppose the "mine" and "thine" that Kant speaks of, in speaking of perceptual apperception (surely one of Kant's most strategically placed distinctions) should function in, for example, Maori experience in precisely the same way it does in Kant's own Königsberg idiom. There's a good deal of psychological and anthropological evidence that shows that the very concept of a self or person — or soul or society, for that matter — is decidedly labile and unpredictably variable among different peoples and even small aggregates of persons within the same informally circumscribed society, in ways that might well threaten to make casual,

---

24 I find the conjecture supported in a thoughtful way by Dan Zahavi, *Mindedness, Mindlessness, and First-Person Authority*, in *Mind, Reason, and Being-in-the-World: The McDowell-Dreyfus Debate*, ed. Joseph K. Schear (London: Routledge, 2013), pp. 320–343. Zahavi is able, by this distinction, to challenge McDowell's strikingly severe version of Kantian rationalism (regarding perception and perceptual judgment) in the *Woodbridge Lectures* (particularly the second lecture) *and* the "correction" McDowell provides in his *Avoiding the Myth of the Given*. Both the *Woodbridge Lectures* and his *Avoiding the Myth* paper appear in John McDowell, *Having the World in View: Essays on Kant, Hegel, and Sellars* (Cambridge: Harvard University Press, 2009), pp. 1–65 and 256–272, respectively. What, in passing, Zahavi demonstrates, is that perceptual awareness is probably, in some measure, reflexively present in sensory awareness itself, without being invoked relationally (as through the accompaniment of discursive thought). McDowell, following Kant, must treat discursive awareness in relational terms (as far as sensibility is concerned, wherever concepts are invoked), which points to the vulnerability of the entire Kantian program. I shall have something to say about Kant's theory of apperception, which I take to be broached in a distinctly primitive and vulnerable form. Nevertheless, as far as I am aware, Zahavi does not pursue the matter of intelligence or cognition (or awareness) among languageless animals. See, further, Dan Zahavi, *Self-Awareness and Alterity: A Phenomenological Investigation* (Evanston: Northwestern University Press, 1999), Chs. 1–2. Thus, Zahavi holds — entirely reasonably — that "nonegological or egoless experiences are *prereflectively* self-aware" (p. 27). (But, of course, that's not to say that, in speaking of what I am thinking of at the moment, I am "aware of myself" in the same sense in which "egoless experiences" are "self-aware.") The "self" is more puzzling than it seems.

random, or adventitious conversation not insignificantly indeterminable and potentially unreliable.

Hence, if it's true that persons are culturally constituted transforms of natural-kind primates (under the condition of learning a contingent local language), then, if a natural language is, similarly, an artifact invented (over an immensity of time) by the sort of artifact we call a person, our understanding one another successfully in spontaneous conversation may come to depend in good measure on the somewhat gratuitous reassurances of inobtrusively (but welcome), imperfectly reliable (but tolerable) additional mongrel conventions and liberties inspired by such a need (whether grammatical, factual, conceptual, theoretical, or philosophical) — readily discerned to function thus, by street-wise speakers enabled thereby to discount more securely (at some small communicative cost) the apparent risks of misunderstanding typical conversational exchanges. We may, then, always be in need of such spongy guarantees, fitted to a "world we can live with," that draws at once on what is passably accurate and adequate and what, though faulty, remains tolerably reassuring when habituated — a quotidian "mid-world" (as I sometimes call it), a schematic and approximative picture of our continually changing experienced world that, on average, functions reliably enough, but cannot be entirely reliable beyond its observed functional range.

It's an important part of my thesis that a considerable run of canonical philosophy (my own conjectures here, as well as Descartes's and Kant's more polished systems) is as much caught up with mongrel proposals as with philosophical truth; also, that the advocacy of deliberate, additional such liberties is itself close to the nerve of pragmatism's skeptical outlook, classic as well as current, regarding the very idea of analytic precision applied to the human world. I cannot see how else to read Descartes's dualism, Kant's apperceptive unity, Peirce's infinitist fallibilism, or Sellars's *agon* involving the "manifest image" and the "scientific image." All four ventures offer problematic economies fitted to important issues, favoring quarrelsome conceptual shortcuts, possible incoherence, inappropriate analogical reasoning and the like, remaining through it all surprisingly reassuring in their mongrel work. None of these maneuvers seems significantly weakened by turning back to their original philosophical settings. That's not where they flourish, however, when they are invoked congenially in conversation. Their seeming defects tend to be nullified by the reassuring efficiencies of whatever enables successful exchange. Ordinary discourse must be continually reassured about its having eluded or overcome misunderstanding, under the extraordinary condition that no one can be quite sure that chance conversations among adventitious participants actually work. Discourse may not succeed on all counts: the world moves too quickly. But savvy conversationalists share any number of reassuring interventions (including mongrel tricks) that enable them to secure a moiety of their original purposes and needs. The rest is expendable noise.

I mention all this, for at least two closely linked reasons: first, to confirm that the mongrel functionality of language actually favors the deep informality of pragmatist philosophy; and, second, to remark that that affinity confirms the unlikelihood that any Fregean-like rationalist venture, such as Brandom's inferentialism (also, perhaps Sellars's somewhat mysterious account of "material inference," which undoubtedly inspired Brandom but was never developed with the conviction and panache of Brandom's own efforts), can possibly be congenial to the principal themes of the classic pragmatist canon (such as it is). Brandom calls himself an "analytic pragmatist," by which he means that he believes that large truth-seeking inquiries (among the sciences and within practical life) must be grounded (at least heuristically, if I understand him rightly) in terms of a "metaphilosophical framework" of argument suitably analogized to the *Begriffsschrift* model. My sense is that Brandom does not actually believe that such a rationalist framework *can* be fully formulated for inquiries addressed to the real world; still, he means (at the very least) to give structural primacy to an inferentialist semantics that, without sacrificing relevance, might be said to enjoy autonomy with respect to data of whatever forms of noninferential observation belong to this or that pertinent empirical inquiry.[25]

According to the pragmatists — Dewey preeminently — the discursive processes of ordinary life and conversational exchange are caught up with what is at least "warrantable" (fitting or workable) under existential circumstances, more than with what is finally said to be strictly "true." That's to say, habituated verbal usage tends to serve a mongrel function if it serves any function at all. "Truth" (for Dewey) is a notably narrower,

---

25   See Brandom, *From Empiricism to Expressivism*, Chs. 3–5; also, Wilfrid Sellars, *Language, Rules and Behavior*, in Jeffrey F. Sicha (ed.), *Pure Pragmatics and Possible Worlds: The Early Essays of Wilfrid Sellars* (Atascadero, 1998, 2005), p. 423: "the mode of existence of a rule [a rule of material inference] is as a generalization written in flesh and blood, or nerve and sinew, rather than in pen and ink".

more technical and specialized matter than "warrantability"[26] — a not uninteresting maneuver on Dewey's part that anticipates conceding the inherently subordinate function of cognizing reason in any wide-ranging account of what to regard as settled knowledge — well beyond the confines of arithmetic.

One begins to see, therefore, that the pragmatist's interest in the mongrel (both classic and contemporary pragmatism) is already of a piece with pragmatism's opposition to any strict Kantian or Fregean (rationalist) ministrations. Brandom, for example, tends to segregate the supposed "pragmatisms" of Carnap, Sellars, and himself from the seemingly more empirical or empiricist "pragmatist" concessions of Dewey and figures like C.I. Lewis and W.V. Quine (and even Wittgenstein). It's for this reason that Brandom says so deliberately, in *Articulating Reasons*:

> Here, I speak with the vulgar, so as to avoid lengthy paraphrase. 'Experience' is not one of my words. I did not find it necessary to use it in the many pages of *Making It Explicit* (though it is mentioned), and the same policy prevails in the body of this work. I do not see that we need — either in epistemology or, more important, in semantics — to appeal to any intermediaries between perceptible facts and reports of them that are noninferentially elicited by the exercise of reliable differential response dispositions [say, the senses].[27]

I must be candid enough to say that, apart from Brandom's venture's being essentially "programmatic" (Brandom's own term), it goes entirely contrary to pragmatism's basic intuition, which the notion of mongrel language effectively captures; furthermore, although we may avail ourselves of Brandom's intriguing proposal, the pragmatists are bound to deny the primacy of inferentialism (in terms of the parity or primacy of empirical and commonsense observation). "Analytic pragmatism" is profoundly opposed to standard pragmatism, though doubtless the two share some themes with one another. The Wittgenstein of the *Investigations* is closer to the pragmatists than to either Brandom or Sellars: *they* (the latter) subscribe to the *scientia mensura* thesis, whereas the pragmatists are

---

26 See John Dewey, *Logic: The Theory of Inquiry* (New York: Henry Holt, 1938), Chs. 1–2. There's a useful discussion of Dewey's distinction between "judgment" and "proposition" matching the uses of "warrantability" and "truth" (addressing Bertrand Russell's misreading of Dewey), in Tom Burke, *Dewey's New Logic: A Reply to Russell* (Chicago: University of Chicago Press, 1994), Ch. 5.
27 Robert B. Brandom, *Articulating Reasons: An Introduction to Inferentialism* (Cambridge: Harvard University Press, 2000), pp. 205–206 (Introduction, n 7.).

committed to the opposed thesis, "man is the measure of what is, that it is, and of what is not, that it is not".[28]

So we allow ourselves the liberty of being reassured (at some tolerable communicative cost) that selected, admittedly faulty, conceptual concessions, sly elisions of fact and fiction and the like, may yet count, conversationally, as harboring, for the nonce, passably acceptable characterizations of the world we inhabit: which is to say, we automatically discount (as conceptually inert) whatever we suppose to be intolerably false or indefensible in what, otherwise, mingles easily with the benefit of believing that our discursive exchanges succeed for the most part in important and relatively urgent cases.

If you doubt the claim, just try to formulate a conception of mind you believe to be strictly true by the straitest tests *and*, at the same time, can be shown to be readily understood by ordinary folk and applied by them in effective ways in ordinary discourse. If you grasp the difficulty, you begin to see in a fresh way the pragmatic genius of Descartes and Kant. (They provide my principal specimens of mongrel philosophy — which is hardly to dismiss them.) I say each is busy, respectively, constructing either a passable dualism or a passable apperceptive unity, that, though philosophically faulty, somehow yields a reassuring picture of our contrived "mid-world," meant to provide a sense of the continually adequate fit between language and world, just where philosophical proposals touch on verbal and conceptual liberties tolerably insinuated into ordinary discourse, without any need for unconditional coherence or consistency or reliable confirmation. (My sense is that it's the plausibility of the usage, rather than the supporting argument, that counts.) Descartes was obviously aware that his affirmed dualism could never be convincingly reconciled with his sanguine belief in the actuality of integrally unitary humans — which are impossible to characterize as assemblies of any kind of aggregated mental and physical attributes. He argues philosophically, but he's remembered mongrelly. That's to say: the piecemeal inadequacies of his specific claims conspire to assure us that a satisfactory theory of the mind is all but there for the taking, though Descartes himself never delivers the goods.

Let me add here what Kant actually says about apperceptive unity — it captures nearly the whole of his theory of the proprietary *Ich* of perception and subjective experience:

---

28   Brandom, *From Empiricism to Expressivism*, p. 15

> The *I think* [the *Cogito*, the *Ich denke*, Kant says] must be able to accompany all my representations, for otherwise something would be represented in me that could not be thought at all, which is as much as to say that the representation would either be impossible or else at least would be nothing for me. That representation that can be given prior to all thinking is called *intuition*... [but] is an act of *spontaneity*, i.e. it cannot be regarded as belonging to sensibility. I call it the *pure apperception*, in order to distinguish it from the *empirical* one, ...I also call its unity the *transcendental unity* of self-consciousness, in order to designate the possibility of *a priori* cognition from it.[29]

It's altogether too easy to read what Kant says here as being no more than tautological: Kant notes, in much the same way Descartes does (regarding dualism), that there must be *some* solution to the apperception problem. But he says next to nothing about the possible merit of alternative solutions; and, of course, given the well-known difficulties of Kant's first *Critique*, if we preferred another picture of the relationship between "sensibility" and "thought," the abstraction we know as the "transcendental *Ich*" might be no more than a minor deflection. (I don't think McDowell's "quietism," in the Woodbridge Lectures, helps us here.) The question is really, at least in part, a matter for an empirically changing psychology — but, then, ultimately, it *is* a conceptual matter.

There is, nevertheless, a misleading simplicity in Kant's notion of a unitary apperceptive site: when we have a strong, reflexively referential impression of a constant self possessing a run of experiences, we assimilate the "whole" of (our) experience or mental life to "it"; though we are often uncertain as to whether a particular memory is indeed "mine" or whether only the mere memory of the reception of its being reported is mine. This, in turn, suggests (perhaps not too far removed from Derek Parfit's speculation) that there is no assured unity in the matter — I would say, in part at least, because persons are artifactual anyway. Unconditional unity, in Kant's sense, does not seem to be the center of the question. Our strongest intuitions seem to be keyed to the would-be principle: "one body, one person." But if you allow the "multiple-personality" phenomenon, even that option is not entirely satisfactory. Here, too, I see a plausible pragmatist

---

29   Kant's account of the apperceptive problem is collected in the Second Section, "Of the Deduction of the Pure Concepts of the Understanding," in the first *Critique*. See Immanuel Kant, *Critique of Pure Reason*, trans. and ed. Paul Guyer and Allen W. Wood (Cambridge: Cambridge University Press, 1998), §§15–27 (B129–169); the passage cited appears at B131–132. Descartes seems not to have formulated the solution to his puzzle, though he gives Princess Elisabeth reason to believe he will provide one.

answer: we need enough unity to accommodate the principal narratives of life and responsibility that we cannot ignore; and what we cannot really recover (early childhood memories and their own narrative unity) we may safely ignore. But then, apperceptive unity is itself constructed as we proceed in life, hardly transcendentally; or, there is an ineliminable touch of tautology in the *Cogito* itself: it does seem to be a mongrel device in both Descartes and Kant as it is in our own discourse.

What, for his part, Descartes flags is the fact that there's a genuine use for both idioms (the dualistic and the integrated), the right use of which (if not inserted as a merely fleeting confession of failure) must be mongrel rather than indubitable, since it flaunts an *aporia*. That's to say, it fails as literal-minded philosophy but succeeds as a defanged reminder of an important conceptual resource of ordinary discourse that has as yet not been adequately reconciled with any seemingly viable account of the mind. I read this as a sign of a satisfactory sort of incipient pragmatism that one finds throughout the history of philosophy.

These issues are clearly more than matters of philosophical failure. I take them, for instance, to explain our persistent interest in both Descartes and Kant: the ultimate resolution of the questions they pose cannot fail to address the distinctions each has featured; yet, the mongrel maneuver simply converts the promise into a shadow of the actual solution, without demonstrating that our assurance is justified factually. My own intuition has it that, in matters like that of the right analysis of the cognitive powers of the mind, the nature and conditions of knowledge, the determinacy of the meaning of what we say, will never be completely satisfied with any non-trivial answers and will oblige every promising formulation to keep adjusting itself to the changing fashion of answering correctly. It's there, of course, that inquiry becomes insuperably reflexive and question begging, and it's there that the pragmatists oppose any form of cognitive confidence beyond what is deemed sufficient for our passing needs. (That's to say: they have very little confidence in any strong reading of the objective standing of an essentialized answer to the question about knowledge.)

Kant, I should add, builds so much authoritative power into his notion of the transcendental *Ich* that its mere mention precludes alternative empirical (and philosophical) possibilities (just the ones, I may as well say, that have exercised McDowell so strenuously — perhaps even futilely). I see no reason, for instance, why the unity of apperception could not be plausibly *imputed* (for practical purposes, even if mistakenly, in the sense in which would-be memories that rightly belong to other persons may be harmlessly but usefully claimed, where they contribute to our own holistic understanding of the matter in question. Once we depart from Cartesian infallibility, it's difficult to follow the actual path of apperceptive unity. The empirical *Ich* may be as much as we can safely confirm. In that sense, Kant's transcendentalism may itself be a mongrel instrument rather than, invariably, a transcendentally infallible guess. In any case, its would-be powers are not entirely convincingly secured.

I also see no objection to conceding that particular perceptions and experiences may be qualified by our discursive powers without actually implicating the active functioning of the *Ich* of perceptual judgment (a thesis the McDowell of the *Woodbridge Lectures* very firmly believed runs contrary to Kant's own view, though it might have been favorably regarded by Sellars). Later, McDowell relents on laxer grounds that he came to regard as still genuinely Kantian, though he remains firm about the need for a thoroughly rationalist solution to the problem of perceptual judgment.[30] In fact, the infant's accomplishment seems to require deeper concessions than these, since the primate creature that begins to acquire language has no cognitive powers of a specifically person-level cast at all.

Here, again, the empirical trumps the transcendental. The infant's unrivaled feat, the admission of perception and experience's being inherently "self-aware" among animals (*a fortiori*, among infants and mature persons), the implausible simplicity of Kant's account of apperception, the reasonableness of conceding perceptually-grounded non-discursive analogues of discursive judgment on the part of the most advanced animals, the possibility of more complex options of cognitively pertinent forms of perceptual cognition on the part of enlanguaged persons — hypnotically-induced amnesia, for instance, regarding the judgmental *Ich*, or the acquisition of collateral information brought to bear on prior perception not yet explicitly processed in the form of perceptual judgment — converge to suggest that *a priori* necessities of the kind favored by Kant and McDowell are probably much more uncertain than either would be prepared to concede. But there's no question Descartes and Kant have no compelling grounds for disallowing robust forms of animal intelligence and nondiscursive cognition.

Ultimately, on my reading, persons become determinate actualities (entities) initially by entrenching fictive referents as the designated sites

---

30 See McDowell, *Having the World in View*, Pt. I (the *Woodbridge Lectures*); and in the same volume, *Avoiding the Myth of the Given*, pp. 256–272. See, also, the opposed papers by McDowell and Hubert Dreyfus, Pt. I of *Mind, Reason, and Being-in-the-World: The McDowell-Dreyfus Debate*, ed. Joseph K. Schear (London: Routledge, 2013).

of self-referential avowal; and then, with maturation and the mastery of language, these nominal or "grammatical" sites evolve as the experiencing sites of proprietary inner experience. Literally, we learn to become aware of ourselves discursively, as experiencing whatever it is we can avow we experience. I view this formulation as a fair rebuttal to Daniel Dennett's well-known, profoundly comic but also self-defeating proposal of persons or selves as no more than delusive spin-offs of wild brain activity.[31] (Dennett advances a clause too many. Hume, I think, was too hasty in his confession. Merleau-Ponty was too sanguine in his confidence in the final legibility of the paradoxes of perception he took with him to the grave.)

The pragmatist's alternative treats all affirmations of what is self-referentially real (or fictional or the like) as constructively labile — forever provisional, artifactual, instrumental, opportunistic, variably interpreted (for local purposes), possibly no more than honorific, or indeed actual (as the proprietary site of sensibility and thought and the like). *If* such affirmations are indeed artifactual and constructivist, then attributions of reality or actuality cannot exceed the assurance of the *Cogito* itself. Where is the ground on which Dennett pretends to stand? The very viability of our cognitive engagement with truth and reality finally lies with (what I've called) the "existential" conviction of the conatus of the human infant and the animal resonances of the human person — not, independently, with the onset of reflexive discursivity at any level of human life. But if you see that, you see as well that the reassurance of the success of mongrel discourse exceeds the self-correction of philosophical mistakes: it's the discernment of the conjectured mistakes that assures us of the accessibility of objective truth, however long the delay may prove to be — not because we have found a significant error on which to build a better theory, but rather because the sources of our engagement with truth and error ultimately lies in the animal sources of the conviction of life itself, *not* in any of our hothouse doctrines. Realism seems to be nearly an ineluctable conviction among humans — compatible, I remind you, with moderate forms of skepticism.[32] It may be hard-wired, in much the same way it is among animals (who cannot pose the skeptical question). I say it's "existential" in *that* sense (*not* actually cognitive) *and* that epistemological questions presuppose and depend upon our animal ardor (the Darwinian factor) — hence, outflank the self-referential paradoxes of First Philosophy. (Not

---

31   See Daniel C. Dennett, *Consciousness Explained* (Boston: Little, Brown 1991).
32   See, especially, Barry Stroud, *Taking Skepticism Seriously*, in *Understanding Human Knowledge: Philosophical Essays*, (Oxford: Oxford University Press, 2006), pp. 38–50.

without our mongrel liberties, however.) Questions regarding the standing of cognition, therefore, are conceptually subordinate to the demands of life itself. (That, too, is a pragmatist conviction, and a metaphysical and epistemological economy that we cannot — and need not — confirm.)

There's the splendid point of Wittgenstein's answer to his own remarkable question:

> 'So you are saying that human agreement decides what is true and what is false?' — It is what human beings *say* that is true and false: and they agree in the *language* they use. That is not agreement in opinions, but in form of life.

To which Wittgenstein adds:

> If language is to be a means of communication there must be agreement not only in definitions but also (queer as this may sound) in judgments. This seems to abolish logic, but does not do so.[33]

My point is that this is as close to the mark as pragmatism or Kantian transcendentalism ever gets, though Wittgenstein was not himself a pragmatist or a Kantian. But there are two prongs to the lesson: one, that there must be some minimal judgments that are compelling enough for a group of speakers to share, that will support "a certain constancy in results of measurement [or cognate operation]"; and the second, that their agreement depends on their conviction in actually sharing a form of life that makes that possible, not the particular judgment or judgments that they happen to share — *a fortiori*, not any. As far as I can see, there is no other way to escape the regressive disappointments of Fregean and Kantian rationalism — and allied claims — the absorption of the "space of reasons" *within* a viable, insuperably local "form of life." That, I suggest is pragmatism's (and Wittgenstein's) ace.

_____

33   Wittgenstein, *Philosophical Investigations*, I, §§241–242.

3.
COLLECTIVE INDIVIDUALS

I

I introduced, toward the end of my second lecture, a mongrel economy obliquely linked to a well-known remark of Wittgenstein's, to which I now return — to which I must return — if I am to make sense of the paradoxes I've barely collected: that is, the artifactuality of persons, the mongrel function of ordinary language, and, now, the posit of collective individuals. I view their shared puzzle as guarding, in an unmarked way, an important threshold of philosophical discovery still buried in the academic sands. (I'm speaking against the impoverishment of our conceptual and factual resources.) I don't believe a direct answer to the evolving question will be quite enough to yield an entirely adequate theory of human culture or of the distinctive life of human persons within our enlanguaged world; but I am persuaded that a suitable theory (for our day) must accord with the main lines of the solutions limned, joined to what I shall add here regarding "collective individuals."

We're bound to favor, I feel certain, a theory addressed to the third paradox, which responds, nominally, to the strange premise — post-Darwin — that affirms that, viewed empirically, the invention and mastery of language and the emergence and evolution of persons are one and the same process. I count that the essential thread of the best prospects of pragmatism's recuperated second life, as well as of Western philosophy in general. It confirms, straightforwardly, for instance, that there cannot be a hierarchically privileged disjunction between transcendental or rationalist and empirical or commonsense truths.

But, then, we must now add that the creation (or *Bildung*) of apt persons presupposes the actuality of linguistically enabled and enabling societies or peoples, that, in collectively sharing an enlanguaged form of life, effectively provide for the second-naturing of their progeny. To master a natural language — itself a cultural artifact — is to be transformed in the way of acquiring competences that cannot be characterized solely in individual or aggregated terms (or exclusively in biological terms). There's the double marvel of linguistic fluency: the primate *homo sapiens* spontaneously transforms itself into a self or person, and, thus transformed, gains, second-naturedly, certain distinctly linguistic (and "lingual") skills (which I name "Intentional," and spell with capital "I"), meaning, by that, that the culturally significant or significative (or semiotically freighted) features of these new skills mark a people's offspring as collectively apt for sharing a "form of life" (preeminently, a true or natural language and what such mastery makes possible). Here, I mean, by "collective" or "collectively" (*gemeinschaftlich*), the ineluctable ability acquired by cultural immersion, of spontaneously mastering the discernible and determinable meanings of the vocabularies (and cognate forms of expression) thus acquired that ultimately gain objective standing on the strength of the imputed authority of the tacit practices of a home society.

Quite opportunistically, then, I simply coopt Wittgenstein's inchoate notion of the *Lebensform*, to advance the post-Darwinian "picture" of the use of a natural language (that I've been championing) that, now, affirms the ineluctable actuality of "collective individuals" — a doctrine canonical philosophy has always treated with great suspicion. You may, if you wish, construe this innovation as a mongrel liberty. In pragmatist terms, it makes little difference whether we construe the "device" as fictional or heuristic or actualist: it follows quite closely my proposals regarding persons. Think, here, of the "mongrel" as a decidedly lax game, logically or conceptually — the pragmatist's speculative proxies — by which (at least) to discount the excesses of Kant's would-be transcendental rigor or the ultimate arbitrariness or analytic vacuity of Kant's *a priori* proposals. There is always, of course, more to be said in any account of "what there is"; but if we insist on necessity and universality, our "conditions of possibility" will be analytic and/or empty (rather than synthetic): that is, if they are not merely possible but logically contingent, "systematic" additions to our account. There are no synthetic *a priori* truths of Kant's description to offer here: if such additions prove useful, they will have been wrongly catalogued as synthetic *a priori*.

I am, in effect, attempting to redefine pragmatism. You will recall that I cited Wittgenstein's stunningly compressed rejoinder to one of his most searching questions, to which he never directly returns — say, for the sake of advising us as to how *we* should answer (if we mean to go beyond his own remark: viz., "[human beings] agree in the *language* they use. That is not agreement in opinions, but in form of life" [§241]). But, of course, the entire heap of notes that comprises the whole of the intuition from which *Investigations* itself springs must count as a sort of running commentary on what Wittgenstein could possibly have meant by a "form of life." I am myself in the business of recommending an alternative (but cognate) reading of Wittgenstein's notion: a *Lebensform*, I suggest, when suitably confined to persons, is, simply, trivially, but momentously (in terms of social practices), the nominalized totality of all the continually evolving processes (and all the contexts enabling the processes) of external and internal *Bildung*, that transform human primates into persons and issue in whatever human societies thereupon do, produce, utter, enact, bring about, and Intentionally manifest.

In this sense, the Wittgenstein of *Investigations* is a first cousin to the pragmatists. Hence, as Wittgenstein himself says, no one can know "in advance" (of acting in accord with any explicitly ventured rule or practice, *or* our "form of life") what would be conformable or required: our actual responses (our *lebensformlich* fluencies) qualify our understanding of how we should answer pertinently! Now, here, Wittgenstein is not too far from the thrust of Peirce's intuitions about the tacit confidence he assigns the unspecifiable but needed resources he calls "abductive," or (indeed) from what Dewey characterizes in terms of his "indeterminate situations." I take this to be a decisive key to the meaning of the epistemological and metaphysical advice of the strongest, most daring forms of pragmatism (and allied convictions) — the ultimate bane of every form of classic rationalism.

The uniquely human world, the enlanguaged natural world — what, for sheer convenience, I nominate the "Intentional world" — is uniquely emergent, in the precise sense that it's irreducible to the physical or material world and cannot be captured dualistically or reductively or atomistically. As with language, it's visible and intelligible only to its privileged creatures — that is, persons, ourselves. Ponder that!

The point of characterizing the human *Lebensform* this way is to ensure the hybrid artifactuality of the whole of the human world, visible, ultimately, only to itself. So that the very question of the existence and actuality of that world (and all that it contains) answers ultimately and entirely to the realist standing of the human person — which, as I say, I treat as a matter of reflexive existential expression (in effect, my reading of what arises before the *Cogito*: Cartesian, Kantian, Husserlian, pragmatist, or other) rather than of any affirmation of incontrovertible self-evidence. Accordingly, all cognitive questions — epistemological, metaphysical, methodological, evidentiary — rely dependently and discursively on our existential (our animal) urgencies.

It's the sheer vitality of animal life — *conatus*, let us say — the primitive force of "self-aware" sensibility (in the animal sense, as I've suggested, drawing on Dan Zahavi's terminology), well below the level of discursivity (*a fortiori*, discursive knowledge) that cannot be ignored by eventual reflection: the animal precursor of the *Cogito* that, as it becomes increasingly palpable and absorbing, makes the cognitive question itself possible — that is, feasibly answerable. What "there is" and what we "can know" cannot resist the growing *existential presence of the evolving self* — not that we know it indubitably, but that its functional ubiquity cannot be denied in acknowledging what we admit within our range of reflexive experience. Cognitive reflection emerges, somehow, out of the reflexive sensibility of animal life. That way, we escape the would-be regress of evidentiary assurances. There's no other way to avoid the obvious paradox. I say that cognition arises out of "self-aware" sensibility whether enlanguaged or not — and I take the sense of such phrasing to count as a possible paraphrase of what Dewey means by an "indeterminate situation." The very robustness of our confidence in the possibility of cognition rests on non-cognitive urgencies: an existential *reductio*.

Thus, we cannot fail to confront the currently fashionable fiddling with Wilfrid Sellars's important "placement" question: it's a decisive question, to be sure, but it's missed by its own promoters: it's not a Kantian (or a Fregean) matter at all (as the Pittsburghers, including Sellars, suppose); it's a matter (let us rather say) of "placing" the Kantian question within the larger space of a *Lebensform*, the ineluctable collectivity within which aggregated individual thought and speech and action prove intelligible at all. Perhaps it's another version of the bridging function of the existential *cogito* that precedes and enables the "true" *Cogito* that Descartes advances — very possibly, then, a tribute to Wittgenstein's eclipsing Kant's pre-Darwinian rationalism (which worried the younger Pittsburghers).

Just review Sellars's wording of the "space of reasons" passage in *Empiricism and the Philosophy of Mind*: no Kantian or Fregean of the Pittsburgh stripe pays much attention to the incommensurability of cultural "holism" or collectivity and Cartesian, Kantian, or Fregean rationalism. But, of course, it's the neglected post-Darwinian (perhaps even distantly Hegelian) theme that makes the reconciliation of Kantian transcendentalism and pragmatism impossible:

> The essential point [about knowledge, Sellars holds] is that in characterizing an episode or a state as that of *knowing*, we are not giving an empirical description of that episode or state: we are placing it in the logical space of reasons, of justifying and being able to justify what one says.[1]

1   Wilfrid Sellars, *Empiricism and the Philosophy of Mind* (Cambridge: Harvard University Press, 1997), p. 76 (§36), reprinted from *Minnesota Studies in Philosophy of Science*, vol. 1, eds. Herbert Feigl and Michael Scriven (Minneapolis: University of Minnesota Press, 1956).

It's very difficult to read this remark without supposing that Sellars meant it to signal the primacy and validity of some form of Kantian rationalism or (perhaps) the Fregean possibilities of the Kantian spirit. Indeed, that may have misled Brandom originally. (Of course, "knowing" is not directly describable perceptually or experientially in any way.) But if the post-Darwinian argument — that views the self or person as an artifactual hybrid yielded by the mastery of a natural language implicates its "placement" within a collective cultural space akin to a Wittgensteinian "form of life" (or a Hegelian "history") — is at all plausible, then Sellars's fashionable phrase cannot escape acknowledging the collective and historied complications of post-Kantian theories of Intentional description and explanation; and, then, transcendental necessity will have been ruled out of play. Classic pragmatism is the principal beneficiary of this line of reasoning. Pragmatism, I should add, is wedded to the animal sources of experience and thought — and to the flux of the world. (Sellars is problematically drawn to both pragmatism and rationalism.)

There's the clue to the distinctive economy I extract from the post-Darwinian discovery of the artifactual standing of persons. I'm prepared to claim that it captures the most plausible strategy for disarming all the regressive circularities of First Philosophy. Beyond that, the actual use of language defines the paradigm of collective existence itself — in the plain sense that to master a natural language is, precisely, to share a language collectively, not merely aggregatively and in historied ways. It's impossible to explain linguistic fluency solely in aggregative terms, though speech, of course, viewed as an action, is primarily assigned individual agents; objective meanings, however, are characteristically construed in collective terms — defeating Humpty Dumpty hands down, let us say. I have no trouble admitting that, initially, collective individuals (societies, peoples, nations, and the like) are undoubtedly fictive; but, as with persons themselves, societies of persons become, by the rote iteration of speech and action, actual — mongrel inventions that require and generate mongrel liberties of their own. The onset of natural language cannot possibly have waited for a satisfactory metaphysics to arrive.

The main source of bafflement (or wonder) in these matters is, I daresay, not entirely distinguishable from Descartes's abiding puzzlement, separated from the arch question of the *Cogito* and centered on the extraordinary contrast between the very different vocabularies of the mental and the physical, now construed (in terms of a narrower but more momentous contrast), emergently, no longer dualistically, involving the difference between the "Intentional" (the enlanguaged cultural) and the physical. It's precisely that complex contrast that we must conjure with if we are to free ourselves, convincingly, from the cognitive pretensions of the great tradition of modern rationalism that Kant himself opposed, which runs, in ever bolder ways, from Descartes to Kant (partly at least against Kant) to Frege, and then spills over (in our time) into the relatively local skirmishes that are involved in our grasp of the ultimate relationship linking Kant and the pragmatists.

I read these linkages in the pragmatist way. In fact, it's the excesses of the neo-Fregeans and latter-day Kantians among us that show the way (unwittingly perhaps) to recuperating pragmatism's second life from its recent regressive temptations — both Kantian and Fregean — tendered by the Pittsburgh School. In effect, it's the Pittsburghers' rationalist longings that finally clarify pragmatism's most promising options in our time.

I'm persuaded that the confrontation between the Kant of the first *Critique* and the classic pragmatists was destined to be the essential contest of late twentieth- and early twenty-first-century philosophy and that each of my would-be paradoxes has had a hand in determining its outcome. I've mentioned Peirce's verdict, that Kant was a "confused pragmatist," which effectively signifies (in Peirce's opinion) that what a literal minded transcendentalism posits is perfect "nonsense," in the sense in which Kant is himself unquestionably aware that we cannot say anything substantive about noumena — although, of course, Kant manages to violate his own rule. This is not to deny the intelligibility of a mind-independent world: what the pragmatist denies is, first, that a posited mind-independent world must (or could) be a noumenal world; and, second, that what we allege is true, transcendentally, of a mind-independent world can ever be known, straightforwardly, to be a synthetic *a priori* discovery.

Anything deemed true of the independent world (according to Peirce's formulation) cannot be *epistemically* independent of the cognizing mind (which of course is Kant's own view as well); accordingly, no realist reading of the world can fail to be conjectural, contingent, interactional, fallible, open to empirical correction, testable (according to our lights) in ways that can never be more than approximative and historied when measured against some pertinent would-be necessary truth. In short, our realist readings must be *constructed*, "ideal" (in the appropriate epistemological sense), though not ontologically and not in any way that would disallow a "realist" reading as well. We cannot distinguish between an *a priori* transcendental and a contingent empirical truth, *if* (as seems evident) the first is itself empirically falsifiable in the light of historied discoveries. Think only of Kant's convictions about the fixed application of Euclid's geometry and Einstein's innovations regarding spacetime. Which is to say: Kant was himself a rationalist of the privileged or dogmatic sort he himself deplores and opposes.

This is the prescient sense in which Peirce treats Kant as a failed or recuperable pragmatist. My own view is that Kant without the apriorist reading of the transcendental is not the true Kant, and that (nevertheless) the latter "Kant" may well be a pragmatist. In that sense, Kant wins and loses by the same maneuver: if the *a priori* is no more than *a posteriori* (possibly in a sense akin to C.I. Lewis's proposal or Hilary Putnam's[2] — or, for that matter, Quine's attack on the analytic/synthetic distinction), then my retrodictive prophecy regarding the convergence of Western philosophy will have been confirmed.

Here I endorse Nicholas Rescher's compelling capture of Peirce's instruction regarding Kant, suited in a particularly trim way to pragmatism's revival in the seventies and eighties:

> Toward transcendental reality itself [Rescher advises], it is appropriate to take much the same stance that Kant took toward his "thing in itself." As such, there is nothing to be said about it: its character is fundamentally a matter of *je ne sais quoi*, because we recognize that definitive and error-immune claims to knowledge cannot be substantiated at the level of scientific theorizing.[3]

It should be clear, then, that to concede this much renders our descriptions *of* the independent world — *qua* independent — imputations separated (on some plausible hypothesis) from other descriptions we take to be relativized to and qualified by the peculiarities of specifically human modes of perception and conception. You see the sense, then, in which our descriptive categories may be said to be "idealist" (in at least two epistemologically distinct respects) and the associated sense in which, nevertheless, true descriptions may be said to be "realist" (now, also, in two distinct *ontological* respects). But to say they are "constructions" is to speak in the epistemological way, even though, post-Kant, epistemology and metaphysics cannot but be inseparable.

Alternatively put: we need not say that we *construct* the "real world" when we treat our categories as idealist (or instrumental) constructions

---

2 See C.I. Lewis, *A Pragmatic Conception of the* A Priori (1923), in *Collected Papers of Clarence Irving Lewis*, eds. John D. Goheen and John L. Mothershead, Jr. (Stanford: Stanford University Press, 1970), pp. 231–239; and Hilary Putnam, *Ethics without Ontology* (Cambridge: Harvard University Press, 2004), pp. 60–65.

3 Nicholas Rescher, *Human Knowledge in Idealistic Perspective: Vol. 1, A System of Pragmatic Idealism* (Princeton: Princeton University Press, 1991), p. 264.

(that nevertheless yield realist attributions). *What* we construct is, rather, a "picture" of the independent world that is both "idealist" *and* "realist" in the seperable senses remarked. We hold fast to Peirce's and Rescher's scruple about noumena and we concede the imputational need to distinguish between descriptions we conjecture "correspond" to the way the independent world "is" (apart from our perceptions and conceptions of it) and to the way in which our descriptions are systematically qualified by what we regard as the local (species-wide) peculiarities of specifically human modes of perception and conception. Both sorts of description, I affirm, are tantamount to constructing "pictures" of the world rather than the world itself. We do of course, on occasion, actually produce or utter novel ingredient "things" that belong to the real world, as in constructing, generating, making cultural artifacts of various sorts (artworks, for instance, and space ships); I freely concede that an equivocation arises whenever we speak of the world-described-in-accord-with-our-categories-and-concepts as possessing realist standing as such — where we admit a disjunction between the realist standing of the world-as-thus-described and the realist intent of our descriptive picture(s) of the independent world. But that's to say we cannot escape the permanent provisionality of realist claims. (Furthermore, such representations are never Rortyan *tertia*.)

I find myself in the middle of a conceptual thicket here. (We're addressing an important clue involving all three paradoxes.) The only way to proceed coherently, I suggest, is to refuse any direct cognitive solution of the realist question: *I* think it more than reasonable to believe that we *have* cognitive access to the independent world "sufficient for our needs," but *not* in any way we could ever prove we do, non-circularly! (We cannot avoid begging the question if we pose it.) The evidentiary work of epistemology is, then, insuperably question begging — though impressively effective, instrumentally. Kant's project is literally impossible: that is positing *a priori* truths about the world before we ever consult the world perceptually or in allied ways. The solution rests with dividing the original question into two and making the epistemological part logically dependent on a prior existential commitment (the *conatus* of our animal energies, we may suppose) that has no epistemological pretensions of its own. Proceeding thus, we draw on whatever pertinent beliefs about the unique evolution and conditions of survival of the human species strike us as yielding a plausible explanation of our actual survival, *but without being able to confirm the fact* under the terms given.

In particular, we are inclined to suppose that the human race could never have survived, lacking (as it does) any functionally effective instincts for survival (as infants) that compare favorably with the instincts of new-born horses, deer, and other herd animals, unless humans were able to compensate for their native inability to survive instinctively, as by learning and sharing information regarding how to survive successfully. The seeming argument is perhaps worthless (on purely formal grounds), but it's also existentially overwhelming. Whatever we guess at in this way binds us to the world as animals — existentially, as I say, prior to any sort of *Cogito*! Evidence is not the issue, Wittgenstein says, similarly, it's our sense of sharing a "form of life" that makes our attention to evidentiary issues possible and productive. Some admission of "collective entities" must, therefore, be conceded.

"Do we have any plausible reason to believe we have cognitive access to the mind-independent world (we believe we inhabit)?" I call this first question a "blunderbuss" — an existential matter, to be sure, *not* a question that can be answered in a way that yields evidentiary satisfaction in support of strict truth or falsity. In this sense, the question is resolved along Darwinian lines or in some other "pragmatically" effective way — fictively, heuristically, by way of animal faith or common sense or something of the sort — very possibly something close to Santayana's conjecture or Dewey's. "Warrantedly," in Dewey's sense, if I understand him correctly. The import of this admission is simply to register the inherently diminished or logically defective sense in which *realist* answers to questions of fact or truth about the way the world *is* — *subaltern* questions of what I call "epistemology proper" — cannot be more than "second-best," that is, cannot be more than a *façon de parler*, existentially (but not otherwise) secured.

We lose nothing by such a conviction; on the contrary, the very coherence of human life requires that we adhere to some form of brute realism (if I may name it thus) that compares favorably with the cognate import of animal intelligence and behavior (whatever we make of that). But it signifies that there can be no incompatibility between realist conviction (of the existential sort) and a measure of skepticism about that same realism. In Deweyan terms, as I've already remarked (in the second lecture), we may be said to judge that the survival of the human race is already part of the reflexive confidence of our form of life: no reflexively existential avowals can claim more than that. They make the artifactual confirmation of objective truth-claims possible but do not (except vacuously) confirm any propositional claims. There's the clue to the puzzle of Descartes's *Cogito*: there's an "affirmation" of life — an inescapable spontaneity — that precedes the seeming self-evident claim — and makes it otiose! We aim at truth, but truth is itself confined within vaguely existential bounds that cannot be made determinate enough to treat the inchoate pre-*Cogito*

"*cogito*" before the onset of the canonical *Cogito* as confirmably or self-evidently true.

The pertinent facts, as I understand them, appear to show that the unique invention of language has actually enabled the race to master questions of specialized knowledge to meet almost any eventuality affecting survival. Now then: suppose we read the foregoing as encouraging and strengthening agentive confidence in and commitment to discursive truth-claims, without prior assurances about the conditions of knowledge. We tell ourselves (let us suppose) that we've probably survived because whatever we've done, in living as we do, must be "good enough [somehow] for all our needs." We have no idea how to test the import of our guesses, but everything we consider appears to support our affirmation of life. Thereupon, we move to focus our attention on exploring the second, the epistemological question, under the auspices of our reflexive absorption in the first affirmation. *In time*, much as the fictive grammatical "I" evolves into the existent self (by continual iteration and self-absorption), so, too, our heuristic world begins to acquire (with supportive corrections) a thicker semblance of realist standing! (Much the same is true of understanding linguistic meanings.)

There is no epistemological circle to fear: a moderate skepticism is entirely compatible with our "second-best" realism. I call *that* complex conviction pragmatism, the point of convergence with a Peirceanized Kant who is all too aware of the extravagance of the original Kant's transcendental claims, which convert Kant himself into the preeminent target of his own *Critique*. Here, we begin to see how the fluent use of ordinary language, which straddles our practical heuristics and an increasingly realist conviction, cannot fail to produce a mongrel sort of functionality at the same time it entrenches our best guesses at a realist grasp of the way the world is (according to our lights). We live, therefore, in a mongrel world, a contrived "mid-world," as I suggest, something of a "shadow" world that is, surely, in part fictional, possibly in some measure false — but "good enough" for our coarser quotidian needs, and endlessly corrigible. It's a world that harbors benign distortions (we may suppose) that we seem able to live with, being unable (as we learn through Descartes) to eliminate completely the huge gaps in what we treat as our treasure of knowledge (say, regarding the nature of mind or of what finally "is real").

Peirce, I imagine, would be entirely willing to treat all of this as insuperably qualified by abductive guesses.[4] That is good enough for my present purposes. In any event, I cannot see how we can do better without

---

4   See my *Toward a Metaphysics of Culture* (London: Routledge, 2016), Ch. 3.

changing our assumptions drastically. If, then, you see the importance of the evolutionary continuum spanning nonhuman and human animals, you see *both* the feasibility of languageless infants mastering language and the inexactitude of ordinary language (on which linguistic precision — whatever that may prove to be — itself depends). Hence, if you suppose, as I do, that we have hardly progressed very far in our understanding of the mental life of humans beyond Descartes's distinction between the general vocabularies of body and mind (which Descartes neatly abstracts from mongrel Latin and mongrel French), you cannot fail to grasp the important fact that the fluencies of natural language hardly confirm — as the evidence makes clear — that we positively require a true and accurate model of mind or knowledge, or of the meaning of words and sentences, or of the true structure of the things of the world. We have endlessly many clever devices for securing a sense of an orderly world "sufficient for all our needs," though still forever open to enlargement and correction.[5] One cannot fail to see that, if all this is reasonably true, then both the Wittgenstein of the *Investigations* and the Frege of the *Begriffsschrift* must be mistaken about the whole of philosophy's function vis-à-vis our grip on mundane truth, ordinary thought, and speech. And if that's so, then Kant (and we) cannot be more than confused pragmatists, and the Pittsburgh philosophers (Sellars, Brandom, and McDowell, chiefly) may be deemed to have gone astray, along different lines — regressively, in the rationalist manner — and decidedly against pragmatist intuitions.

The cartoon disjunctions of analytic, continental, and pragmatist philosophies have largely subsided in our young century: in good part, I suppose, as the upshot of Richard Rorty's wayward verdict on philosophy's ultimate futility. The better clue — more accurately, the probable site of a better clue — is already inertly captured in Descartes (apart from the easily misunderstood *Cogito* and its default dualism). I read Descartes as having yielded to much the same mongrel vocabulary that we ourselves support, together with its "shadow" world (or grammar) — that is, rather than as having hit on a particularly clever metaphysics.

Thus, for instance, when we speak of "the language of thought" modeled on ordinary speech (say, in the manner of Peter Geach or Anthony Kenny, regardless of how literally either may intend his notion), it's simply inapt to complain that the bare posit is no more than a mistaken thesis about the

---

5   I must mention again Nicholas Rescher's account of the "realist" and "idealist" aspects of our cognitive grip on the world, though I think I am less sanguine (than Rescher is) about the "realism" of our realisms. See Rescher, *Human Knowledge in Idealist Perspective*, Pt. IV.

metaphysics of thought — or, for that matter, about the supposed structural similarities of human and computer-generated speech. All that's needed is the modest admission that we're genuinely puzzled about the nature and structure of the mind and therefore treat all of our characterizations of the "content" of the mind in heuristically (or "instrumentally") suitable ways — "adequate for all our needs." We simply eschew any strong metaphysical claims. In my lingo, we've introduced a "mongrel" liberty or model, and habituated usage begins to justify the bare incipience of the apparently realist standing of our practice. I see no reason why the "fictionality" of the model cannot come to support the effectively realist functionality of the practice itself. I find a distinct parallel in the potential fictionality of "successful" explanatory models pressed into service in the boldest theories of advanced physics.[6]

Descartes *has* no resolution of the mind/body puzzle at all — effectively, *no one really does*! The best he offers is the pale advice that we should not deny the integral unity of a human life, among the mongrel phrasings we find ourselves attracted to. If that is indeed the ubiquitous, standard practice of ordinary discourse, then Descartes — fortunate man — is not far behind Kant in addressing the supposed "conditions of possibility…" of apperception; for Kant elevates Descartes's *Cogito* as fulfilling the apperceptive function of the Transcendental *Ich*. Viewed thus, the entire point of Descartes's elaborate philosophical gloss on what is really the bare heuristics of mongrel discourse is simply that the unsatisfactory dualism of the mongrel idiom (read philosophically) need not ever defeat its merely practical adequacy and efficiency when its particular phrasings are implicitly recognized as nonce placeholders for whatever may come to persuade us are conceptually better solutions of our interminable puzzles. The fact remains that our verbal inefficiencies serve us even where we cannot yet surmount our ignorance — as in our theories of mind. There's the true merit of the brilliant modesty of perpetual pragmatism. When,

---

6   Even as I write, a recent number of *The Monist* (99, 2, July 2016), 225–322, has acknowledged much the same question (unevenly pursued), under the title "Scientific Fiction-Making." I wish only to emphasize that the practice is well-nigh unavoidable in both history and advanced physics. Why should it be ruled out in psychology and the analysis of thought and speech? I take the question to be more or less the unspoken nerve of Vincent Descombes's stately study, *The Mind's Provisions: A Critique of Cognitivism*, trans. Stephen Adam Schwartz (Princeton: Princeton University Press, 1995). I find something of the same intuition in the "ideal-type" comparisons favored by Max Weber. Have a look at Chapter 1 of Stephen W. Hawking, *A Brief History of Time: From the Big Bang to Black Holes* (New York: Bantam Books, 1988).

therefore, Peter Geach speaks of thought as "saying in one's heart that...
",[7] it makes no serious difference to the fortunate fluencies of ordinary
speech whether we treat the formula as metaphoric, heuristic, fictive, or
philosophically valid (up to some imagined measure of adequacy): it never
loses its mongrel role — because our alternatives can hardly do better and
it is itself (in that sense) "as good as we need." (In fact, I take Descartes's
"third" intuition about the functionally integrated human organism to be a
more sensible posit than Kant's non-human Transcendental *Ich*.)

It's part of my argument that we are quite aware that a considerable
number of our most persistent questions are, on familiar grounds,
interminable and question begging, and even at times inherently impossible
to resolve in any reasonably determinate way. Here, I include *all* questions
of an epistemological cast (as in coming to know *facts* about the world or to
understand the *meanings* of what we say or do as competent persons). There
is, I claim, no independent way to know what knowledge or understanding
is — a way that does not presuppose the very knowledge in question;
although to admit that much need not disallow answers of an acceptably
diminished kind — "second-best," as I call them, solutions that answer to
our "second-natured," emergent resources (the work of a given society's
Bildung), in accord with which the primate members of the species are
transformed into persons, who, *as a consequence*, normally function as
cognitively, linguistically, agentively apt. (Plausible conjecture is all we
need here — and all we can claim.)

That's to say, we acquire (we believe we acquire) the enlanguaged
competencies we claim to have acquired as a result of our prolonged
immersion in the language and culture of our home society. All of our
artifactually emergent competences presuppose our successful immersion
and are (we concede) *inexplicable apart from that*. Accordingly, *their*
validation — in effect, the would-be validation of meanings rightly assigned
any and all of the usual utterances of any natural language — will appear to
be question begging to anyone who believes there must be an independently
valid theory of determinate linguistic meaning that does *not* presuppose or
depend on the criterial application of what counts as knowing the meaning of
all well-formed utterances of the language in question. The trouble with the
immersion theory is said to rest with its being irretrievably question begging.
I think that's true, though it's also rationally tolerable — and inescapable.
The obvious counter-proposal — Donald Davidson's, most famously — is
to devise a theory of how meaning may be linguistically determined from

---

7   See Peter Geach, *Mental Acts* (London: Routledge & Kegan Paul, 1957).

other properties of settled language that may be successfully invoked and do not directly invoke knowledge of the actual meanings of any utterances in the target language. There are no entirely convincing candidate theories here — in, say, the work of W.V. Quine or Alfred Tarski or others — though Davidson requires such a resource.

What Davidson cleverly shows is that Quine's behavioral strategy for translating the utterances of an alien language (the well-known "Gavagai!" example) does not actually address the *interpretive* question Davidson rightly poses — the question of confirming whether Quine has ever actually caught the *meaning* of the expression ("Gavagai!", let's suppose) *in the alien language* he encounters; or, for that matter, whether Quine can ever show that *he understands the meaning of what he himself says in his own language*! I take it that Davidson's cleverness *does not show* that there must be (or even could be) a theory of the kind he claims to require — and thereupon, disastrously, begins to examine. Davidson's project is generally acknowledged to fail completely. Reference to the conditions of immersion does not, in any sense, yield a theory rightly fitted to any operative rule of interpretation; careful studies of Davidson's account of what he calls "radical interpretation" (in contrast to Quine's notion of "radical translation") uniformly conclude that his attempt at an evidentiarily adequate answer is, simply: "impossible".[8]

My own sense of the matter is that the emergence of true language is the emergence of a uniquely novel competence that cannot, in principle, be adequately described, explained, or interpretively applied to specimen utterances, except in its own terms (in effect, circularly). There cannot be any pertinently reductive account in nonlinguistic terms; linguistic meaning cannot be determinately derived from the theory of any other important linguistic property ("translation," for instance); and the vagaries

---

8   There is a massive search regarding the bare feasibility of Davidson's proposal
     provided in Ernie Lepore and Kim Ludwig, *Donald Davidson: Meaning, Truth,
     Language, and Reality* (New York: Oxford University Press, 2005): see, particularly,
     "Summary of Part III," pp. 420–424; the verdict ("impossible") appears at p. 424.
     See, also, Donald Davidson, *Radical Interpretation*, in *Inquiries into Truth and
     Interpretation*, 2nd ed. (Oxford: Clarendon, 2001), pp. 125–139. Quine's view of
     "radical translation" appears in *Word and Object* (Cambridge: MIT Press, 1960), Ch.
     2 (p. 28). See, also, William P. Alston, *Quine on Meaning*, in *The Philosophy of W.V.
     Quine*, eds. Lewis Edwin Hahn and Paul Arthur Schilpp (LaSalle: Open Court,
     1986), pp. 49–75, for a critical reading of Quine's theory; and Ian Hacking, *The
     Parody of Conversation*, in Ernest LePore (ed.), *Truth and Interpretation:
     Perspectives on the Philosophy of Donald Davidson* (Oxford: Basil Blackwell,
     1986), pp. 447–458, for a critical account of phases of Davidson's theory of language.

and vaguenesses of actual meaning cannot be expected to be captured by any determinate theory of Tarski's sort (as developed by Davidson) or by anything akin.

To put the paradox in the baldest way: we understand the meaning of what we say in ordinary discourse, because we are, from infancy up, thoroughly immersed in mastering language, which is itself a uniquely fashioned competence that we are unable to capture in terms of any reductive analysis. If you say. "But that's just begging the question," you see at once both how you cannot better the finding and how that changes, fundamentally, our picture of what we're able to do with science, philosophy, and practical life. But *that*, I suggest, is as close as we can possibly come to isolating the nerve of pragmatism, the convergence of Kantian and pragmatist thinking, the final defeat of rationalism, the recovery of the main thread of classic pragmatist instruction, and related puzzles.

I think you must see how, without explicit elaboration, a fresh theory of the interpretation of meaning — verbal or "lingual," let us say: that is, non-verbal but dependent on the mastery of language, as in the ballet, making love, baking bread — arises from the slim concessions already elicited regarding mongrel language; also, therefore, a cognate lesson regarding the whole of practical life that will require whatever our theory of enlanguaged culture will require, if we are to make sense of the human world itself. The suggestion I wish to put before you is that a frank fiction may be the best we can provide — and that *that* appears to be quite enough for "all our needs," without leading us astray. There's the ultimate point of my third paradox: we understand the meanings of what we say, because we share the form of life in which the question of their validity arises *and* is answerable — and answered. Immersion is not itself an evidentiary matter.

Now, to offer an aside on linguistic meaning (as in accounting for the interpretation of artworks and history) is to insist on the profound informality of the very ability to find and grasp the meaning of whatever belongs to the world of human culture; and, if that's true, then there's bound to be a strong need for the continual provision of mongrel devices in proceeding efficiently in a great deal of ordinary discourse. Here, the very idea of determinate linguistic meaning is unlikely to be causally regular or nomological or algorithmic in any familiar way: we require and depend on fluency, but linguistic fluency is linked to a familiarity with an immensely complex motley of distinctions informally tethered to the contingencies of immersion itself. The same confession already appears in Cassirer, who, however, always insists (*pro forma*) on the vestige of the Kantian "regulative" principle of science, though his own intellectual sweep defeats its steadfastness. (This is another largely neglected matter.)

Earlier, I linked the need for mongrel discourse to our lack of inventive clues about the nature of the entire realm of mind, which has changed very little (in this regard) since the seventeenth century at least. I've also touched on the seemingly endless need for useful (generally unconfirmable) guesses about what is involved in our epistemological and metaphysical conjectures regarding the would-be structure of knowledge and the world we claim to know. We need a sense of the stability of reference and predication in all of this, even where out practice may be largely approximate, transient, fictive, distorted, even false and inaccurate. That, I suggest, does not mean that our ordinary claims lack realist standing: it's rather that "realism" proves to be an extremely modest, sometimes rather protean notion, dependent on (that is, subaltern to) a distinctive kind of existential confidence.

II

I want, now, to go a step or two beyond what I've said about the artifactuality of persons and true language. What I've said thus far is, roughly, this: first, that the process of inventing and mastering language is essentially the same as the process of transforming human primates into persons (what I've called external and internal *Bildung*) — accordingly, that the human person is a hybrid creature not adequately described in *natural-kind* terms alone, without yet exceeding *natural* powers in any way; and, second, that whatever is emergently and uniquely novel in the way true language is cannot be rightly understood except by way of one or another form of Intentional immersion (original or derived) in the culture of the enlanguaged society in question — accordingly, that some dimensions of the human form of life are not (except by way of quarrelsome analogy at the least margin of comparison) shared with other creatures: chiefly, linguistic and lingual meaning, normativity, discursivity itself, historicity, and the Intentionality that signifies the semiotically freighted, emergent import of human actions and societal practices (including speech but not restricted to speech).

Persons or selves, we may say, anticipating the full thrust of the issue, are not simply "individuals" or "individuatable things" (or beings or organisms), in the merely logical sense that ranges, without let, over whatever may be counted and deemed to be actual: or, in the richer, more complex (though still insufficient) sense in which an intelligent organism is identifiable as the same (continuously existing) agent of pertinently linked responses to stimuli that bear directly on its holistic (telic) concerns with survival and flourishing; or, indeed, in the additionally enriched sense in which the second option (just given) is raised up to count as instantiating an integral continuum of the phases of a semiotic or semiotized process of individual life manifested in episodes of pertinent action and response. Such an ordered sequence of possibilities approaches, rather nicely, to Charles Peirce's conception of what it is to be an individual organism of distinct intelligence, without yet distinguishing what it is to be an individual person or self. Peirce seems to have been concerned, over a good part of his career, with formulating a notion of "logical individuality," which, suitably enhanced, might capture as well what may be termed "organismic individuality" (or the individuality of organisms and intelligent agents), without specifically accommodating the individuality of persons or selves. "An individual," Peirce characteristically affirms, "is something which reacts".[9] (He's speaking of the individuality of organisms.)

Of course, Peirce does not neglect the self; it's only that he tends to separate the analysis of the self or person and the analysis of organismic individuality. The reason for the seeming disjunction lies with the perceived need to separate the merely "logical" issue (individuality) from Peirce's plan to bind his theory of the self to answering, systematically, a number of more substantive questions about reasoning, about the distinction between "absolute truth and what you do not doubt," about the new direction of pragmaticism, and, most ambitiously, about construing the purposive career of an individual self — viewed as itself an embodied sign (within a semiotic process), in search of a form of communion with other (say, a potentially infinite company of) signs (*or* selves!) — in a way opposed to the unattractive "selfishness" (the all-but-"illusory" individuality) of "personal minds"(William James's phrase). Quite a basketful, but much too much to attempt to review here.[10]

I allow myself no more than a single citation from Peirce, which serves well enough to clarify Peirce's florid but thoroughly ingenious application to his own questions: primarily because, serendipitously, it also goes some

---

9   *Collected Papers of Charles Sanders Peirce*, eds. Charles Hartshorne and Paul
     Weiss (Cambridge: Harvard University Press, 1931-1935; 1958), 3.613. I
     acknowledge here a considerable debt to Vincent M. Colapietro, *Peirce's
     Approach to the Self: A Semiotic Perspective of Human Subjectivity* (Albany:
     SUNY Press, 1989), especially Chs. 2, 4.
10   See Colapietro's account of Peirce's response to James's views regarding the self
     (drawn from James's *Principles of Psychology*), in *Peirce's Approach to the Self*,
     pp. 61–65.

distance toward explaining the concept of "collective individuals" (which I must in any event provide for my own purposes), in the face of considerable professional resistance (to such conjectures). This may be Peirce's most extended and perspicuous clue regarding the compatibility of speaking of a "society of selves" as itself a "collective individual," within the confines of which individual selves, otherwise aggregated, may be coherently regarded as the proper "parts" of such an individual. I don't believe (but I don't really know whether) Peirce returns to the "logical" option I mean to broach here. But he offers two distinctions:

> The first is that a person is not absolutely an individual. His thoughts are what he is "saying to himself," that is, saying to that other self that is coming into life in the flow of time. When one reasons, it is that critical self that one is trying to persuade; and all thought whatsoever is a sign, and is mostly of the nature of language. The second thing to remember is that the man's circle of society (however widely or narrowly this phrase may be understood), is a sort of loosely compacted person in some respect of higher rank than the person of an individual organism.[11]

I venture two preliminary observations here, in anticipation of an argument I have yet to provide. The first is to draw your attention to the plain fact that Peirce is effectively engaged in proposing a deliberate *mongrel* liberty in addressing a philosophical distinction that he needs but cannot persuasively advance by way of any known canonically acceptable conceptual strategy, though the distinction between a collective and an aggregative society is a commonplace (thought to generate an impermissible contradiction). Peirce avails himself of a bit of verbal trickery here (which we shall soon find to be all but identical with the verbal liberty the well-known sociologist/anthropologist Marcel Mauss employs in much the same circumstances). The other is to draw your attention to Peirce's heterodox treatment of the self — in terms both of introducing the seemingly coherent conceptual option of a continual run of adventitious, finite, overlapping "selves" that may even be thought to be in passing conversation with one another, within the actual career of an individual person (which brings to mind Derek Parfit's well-known proposal), as well as the possibility of a considerable weakening of any strict marks of individuality regarding ordinary selves — as a consequence of mastering the semiotic fluencies of a shared natural language.

I view the liberty of this second strategy as approaching a definite

---

11   *Collected Papers of Charles Sanders Peirce*, 5.421

challenge to Kant's own extremely lax, almost undefended formulation of his theory of apperceptive unity (in both the first *Critique* and the *Prolegomena*), bearing on the presumed (but unsecured) apriority of Kant's "*Ich denke*". Peirce's speculation is more or less empirical rather than *a priori* (in effect, pragmatist: effectively opposed to any rationalist necessity regarding the constant presence of the apperceptive *Ich* in cognitional contexts). I've touched on the matter in the preceding lecture, but now we begin to see the deeper contest between rationalism and pragmatism. (I think there cannot be a rationalist pragmatism that adheres to the concerns of the classic pragmatists, that strengthens the would-be enabling claims of Descartes, Kant, or Frege.)

I take these concessions to entail a form of objectivity (or objective truth) that inherently depends on the ultimate and exclusive service of human judgment (and existential interests), in a sense that discourse about brute nature is thought not to support. The meaning of one of Shakespeare's sonnets, for instance, is entirely a matter of the *bona fides* of competent readers, in a sense in which the causal explanation of the formation of the moon is not. There may be poems too difficult for this or that reader to understand, but none inherently unfathomable within the cultures in which they are produced. Yet it's entirely possible that there be mysteries in nature that we may never understand: though, even there, to admit that much is hardly to agree with Colin McGinn that, say, the phenomenon of consciousness is simply beyond our ken. What counts as knowledge is itself a constructive posit: there are no foundational questions concerning cognitive powers; the issue can never elude its own *petition* — though even that admission is ultimately benign. Hence, if attributions of knowledge are plausible constructions (as I've suggested), then strict versions of *a priori* apperception may be both unnecessary and indemonstrable; and if that is conceded, then the first *Critique* must utterly collapse.

Nevertheless, both because the formulation of the causal question presupposes discursivity (and more) and because the realist standing of the causal question ultimately depends (as I've explained) on the "existential" (*not* any epistemologically defined) import (among reflectively apt persons) of their sheer self-recognition. (Call that the *Cogito*, if you wish, though it's closer to what I'm calling the existential or original "*cogito*"), it's impossible to disjoin the objective standing of the causal issue from the *faute de mieux* privilege of the Intentional world. Which is to say: ascriptions of objective truth belong exclusively to human persons (as things now stand), even though the confirmatory grounds of truth bearing on brute nature cannot rightly be cast in just those terms. The very notion of truth is, ultimately, an expression of hybrid confidence — as much animal as personal — among humans. (Pragmatism at its leanest!)

The physical world is not "bound" to conform with whatever *we* suppose it's like; but despite whatever mistakes we make in reading or interpreting Shakespeare's sonnet, it cannot have a meaning utterly unlike what apt readers judge it to be. Conceivably, the micro-theoretical world of physics may be entirely unimaginable to us, even if we understand the best guesses of advanced physics; but there couldn't be anything comparable in English poetry or history.

Inasmuch as human language is unique, irreducibly emergent in the way it is — as is, also, whatever is "Intentional" (culturally significant or significative) in the sense I've coined — the "things" of the specifically human world are intelligible and discernible *and* actual (as such) *only* to its artifactual denizens: that is, persons. That fact alone signifies — among an array of interesting consequences — that there is nothing strange in admitting the actuality of thoughts and meanings, minds and institutions, numbers and nations. The admission helps explain how it's possible that persons can evolve, through the exercise of linguistically enabling cultural powers, from grammatically fictive sites judiciously selected within the biosphere. But if so, then, of course, reductive materialisms and allied doctrines cannot be adequate to our conceptual needs; it makes more sense to think of the physical sciences as deliberately restricted cognitional instrumentalitities drawn from the conceptual resources of the human sciences and practical life than to regard the human sciences as themselves problematic attenuations of more foundational physicalist vocabularies.

I take the option to be close to the true meaning of the "*Cogito*" (and, therefore, close to the alleged apperceptive work of Kant's "*Ich denke*"). But then, to pursue the matter in terms of the contingencies of a post-Darwinian treatment of persons is to entrench our natural doubts about the strict necessities of Kant's rationalist reading of the categories of the understanding (mentioned in the *Prolegomena*). There, Kant insists that there is no feasible alternative to his apriorism — but there *is* always at least the pragmatist alternative I've been sketching (from Peircean and Deweyan sources)![12] In the natural world, reason is not an autonomous cognitive faculty of any kind.

---

12   Compare Brandom's attempt to reconcile his "analytic pragmatism" with Huw Price's treatment of "object" and "subject naturalism" in an effort to preserve his rationalist (more or less Fregean) reading of pragmatism. See Robert B. Brandom, *From Empiricism to Expressivism: Brandom Reads Sellars* (Cambridge: Harvard University Press, 2015), pp. 90–96; and Huw Price, *Naturalism without Mirrors*

Epistemological responsibility is unique to persons; and the difference between the human primate and the human person is so extraordinary that I find it important to provide a distinctive ontology for persons in order to flag the difference. Normally, for example, we don't assign legal responsibility to any creature that is not a competent person: that constraint, then, significantly affects our theory of action. An action — a deliberate or intentional or purposive action — cannot be a merely bodily movement (as theorists like Davidson and Arthur Danto sometimes affirm);[13] there are too many "Intentional" complications to consider. It helps to be able to say that actions (thus conceived) are embodied or incarnate *in* bodily movements, rather than identical with them, just as we might similarly say that persons are incarnate in certain kinds of primates, or words in uttered sounds, or paintings in painted canvases. Otherwise, difficulties arise involving a reasonably uniform conception of causality, causal laws, motivation, choice, responsibility, and so on.

It wouldn't trouble me at all if you insisted that persons were fictions and linguistic meanings didn't exist in the way the physical world exists, so long as you also acknowledged that if the cultural world does not exist in the way the physical world does, then *the fact that* it's still an "actual" world rests *entirely* with the "fictional" persons who (in the meantime) have "made it" existentially! To say the least: it's more than problematic to deny our own existence, as persons, creatures capable of making truth-claims and of confirming and disconfirming this and that. Here, for instance, I've deliberately invoked a "mongrel liberty": I've treated persons (and would similarly treat artworks and actions) as indissolubly incarnate (and emergent) within the *materiae* of physical nature — essentially as a convenient and viable *façon de parler* — which may be proposed in as literal or heuristic or fictive a way as you please, so long as it permits us to address the distinctive complexities of Intentionally interpretable "things" within the same logical space.

(Oxford: Oxford University Press, 2011); and *Expressivism, Pragmatism, and Representationalism* (Cambridge: Cambridge University Press, 2013). (Brandom's p. 91 n 57 suggests something of the complexity of his own option.) To be candid: I read all quarrels about objectivism, reductive materialism, realism, representationalism, rationalism, naturalism, inferentialism and the like as entirely subaltern or *dependent* options (epistemologically and/or metaphysically); whereas the contest between Kantianism and pragmatism is not a subaltern matter. The question of what it is to be a person is ineluctably central to the whole of philosophy. To dismiss or discount the self or person is always (as in Hume and, may I add, Kant) to go completely astray.

13   See my *Toward a Metaphysics of Culture*, Chs. 1, 2.

But now, finally, I must make room for the paradox of collective individuals. Vincent Descombes, who offers an arresting (but, I think, ultimately unsatisfactory) account of "collective individuals" (specimens of what the lexicographer H.W. Fowler calls "nouns of multitude": *army, Government, party, crowd, tribe, company, people*) fails to address the laxities I've been collecting (in order to lay the ground for a useful liberty), under the condition of the perceived (if transitory) needs of ordinary discourse. Descombes opposes applying any "atomistic" model to the analysis of the collective "things" of the human world, but he remains a somewhat old-fashioned formalist about the usage of ordinary language. (I intend him no slight here, but we've passed the point of his sort of semantic complaints.) He begins with a genuinely intriguing distinction noticed by Bertrand de Jouvenal in translating into French some of Edmund Burke's political prose. For, as it turns out, in putting "*peuple*" for "people" (reasonable enough), Jouvenal flags the elementary fact that "*peuple*" is normally singular (in French) whereas "people" (in English) may be either singular or plural. So that Jouvenal finds himself obliged to use "the solecism '*le peuple sont*' [in the phrasing] 'the people of these colonies *are* of English descent,' (*le peuple de ces colonies sont* (sic) *de descendance anglaise*)."[14] (Descombes does not venture a political analysis here, though he apparently believes the French grammar influenced the Napoleonic form of the State!) His own analysis is meant to be grammatically formal (in a sense akin to the spirit of Wittgenstein's holism, in *Investigations*). But Jouvenal's translation needs no apology: it's a normal verbal liberty — a mongrel liberty (if you please) — not an impropriety of any sort. To have tracked the presence of actual persons to their source in a grammatical fiction is already to have validated the mongrel introduction of "collective individuals," if and where needed! The practice needs only to be explained, wherever readers or speakers may be puzzled.

Thereupon, Descombes turns away from an ordinary conversational liberty, to offer what proves to be a faulty bit of philosophical semantics addressed to the analysis of a marvelously opportune specimen remark provided by Marcel Mauss, that originally suggested the paradox of "collective individuals" to Louis Dumont, which Descombes then attempts to resolve. Now, I want to endorse the propriety of Descombes's *philosophical* intervention (against Wittgenstein's advice against such interventions, cited in my second lecture), but *not* Descombes's intended

---

14   Vincent Descombes, *The Institutions of Meaning: A Defense of Anthropological Holism* (Cambridge: Harvard University Press, 2014), pp. 124–125.

resolution, which (to be candid) is somewhat flatfooted. Here, then, is Mauss's remark (supplied by Descombes):

> A society is an individual; other societies are also individuals. Among them, it is not possible for as long as they remain individualized to build a higher-order individuality. Utopians generally turn a blind eye to this factual and commonsense observation.

Dumont (Descombes reports) notes the paradox; actually, Dumont says very carefully: "It may appear that there is a logical inconsistency in the conjunction of the two aspects: how can a collection of individuals be at the same time an individual of a superior order?" (Of course, Mauss supposes the paradox is entirely benign. His choice of terms is, you will have noticed, strangely similar to Peirce's — on much the same matter.) Descombes then offers his own inflexible analysis:

> if there is to be a society, it must be an individual made up of individuals [he actually has the frontispiece of Hobbes's *Leviathan* in mind] and therefore a collective individual. But the notion of a collective individual contains within it a latent contradiction. On the one hand, we are supposed to imagine a multiplicity that contains enough diversity to justify the adjective "collective." On the other hand, we want to imagine an individual, something that presents itself as undivided and indivisible.

Descombes's answer to the puzzle is that "there is indeed an incoherence and that a collection of individuals can in no way be held to be 'an individual of a superior order'".[15]

Now, I think the right solution is perfectly elementary: read in terms of the usual mongrel tolerance of ordinary discourse, *although* if Mauss's remark were construed literally, it would be self-contradictory and incoherent, the defects in question are easily recognized as deliberate liberties and summarily overridden for the sake of obviously useful and seemingly valid distinctions that it might otherwise be difficult or impossible (for the occasion) to convey by way of standard conceptual devices adequate and ready at hand. No one could fail to recognize that Mauss's expression, a "higher-order individuality" is itself a mongrel signal (possibly a lame one, though it does the trick) meant to *discount the contradiction* as an

---

15   Descombes's treatment of the matter appears largely in *The Institutions of Meaning*, Ch. 5, pp. 123–129 (§1.5). The passage from Mauss appears at p. 126. Dumont's comments appear at pp. 126–127 (including pp. 126–7n8; and Descombes's analysis (cited) appears at p. 127. Descombes supplies the full bibliographical references.

unavoidable inconvenience. Here, I remind you that it cannot be true that ordinary discourse possesses a full set of unconditionally satisfactory conceptual solutions for all the puzzling distinctions philosophers may have failed to provide — and that, as already remarked, this is entirely obvious from the briefest review of the pertinent theories of figures like Descartes, Hume, and Kant. Read in the mongrel way, a philosophical gap does indeed remain to be filled, but it no longer counts as a troublesome contradiction or incoherence. It's a liberty that relieves us of a putatively unnecessary burden.

Call it a "pragmatic" device, if you wish: a small nuisance among the fluencies of ordinary language. I don't view that usage as itself a piece of philosophical work. But it subtends an important discovery nevertheless (overlooked by Wittgenstein, as I've said), namely, that conceptual errors are benignly entrenched in ordinary discourse and invite philosophical correction (where possible). What links the outlook to pragmatism proper is the independent fact that pragmatism adopts a thoroughly instrumentalist approach to the solution of philosophical puzzles, especially those that feature epistemology and metaphysics, philosophical semantics or First Philosophy. That's to say: it favors non-apriorist, non-absolutist, non-essentialist, contingent, provisional, passing, opportunistic, historied, pluralistic, possibly incommensurable, possibly even incompatible solutions, without ever supposing that there are any uniquely correct solutions to such puzzles. They're *heuristic* devices that we treat as capturing a "state of affairs" that we cannot capture verbally except in the mongrel way. (Such devices acquire public standing.)

What I wish to emphasize is that it's the pragmatist's conception of the inherent informality of its instrumentalist treatment of philosophical semantics that might have spared Descombes the futility of his super-rationalist inflexibilities. He's obviously persuaded that if the contradiction or incoherence (of "collective individuals") can never be resolved in the putatively timeless present of some privileged "logical space," then the mongrel use of the offending phrase *in* the temporal flow of ordinary discourse, speakers' intentions, and the acknowledgement of plausible contexts of conversation can never override the uncompelling rigidities of the first! But, I must warn: if Descombes's philosophical practice were indeed the rule, we would hardly be able to speak at all. Effectively, Descombes is recommending that if an apparent contradiction of the sort he addresses occurs, and if it cannot be resolved within his timeless logical present, then either we must unconditionally abandon speaking of nations, peoples, tribes, societies, Governments and the like (as anything other than aggregative), or we must speak of them as indissoluble, holist (collective) entities — which, of course, goes against our purpose. What *we* want to salvage is the fact that, in speaking of "speaking a natural language" or of "fighting a war," we are speaking of discernible facts about the human world itself that we seem unable to invoke without generating what Descombes regards as inadmissible absurdities and contradictions. *We* want to resolve the matter differently. Descombes believes it's impossible to do so.

Descombes rejects the maneuvers suggested — as "ideologies": he's unwilling to admit them as benign (and useful) mongrel liberties that (suitably flagged or habituated) would allow us to treat them as licit, even if we cannot eliminate the obvious infelicities everyone is aware of. As I've already suggested, it's Descartes's inability to formulate a satisfactory answer to Princess Elisabeth's question that justifies (for the time being) the mongrel use of his dualism! Otherwise, someone is bound to say that the first of the great moderns was simply stupid, in that he never abandons his dualism. That cannot be right. Descartes needs the dualism in order to speak of the mind/body puzzle at all! But, as I've been insinuating, if we allow the verbal "liberty" but not the philosophical "blunder" (as I think we must: they are one and the same), then we begin to appreciate the extraordinary corrective power of pragmatism's instrumentalism.[16] I take that to be the key to the *agon* between pragmatism and Kantian rationalism. But, then, I also take the "mongrel turn" to put Brandom's "rationalism" (his inferentialism applied to pragmatic contexts) at mortal risk, since to heed the import of the mongrel liberty is pretty well to construe a very large part of the inferentialism Brandom wishes to add to our interpreted logic ("material inference," in Sellars's idiom) as almost entirely ad hoc and distinctly improvisational.

The "ideology" in question — which Dumont takes Mauss to be attempting to explain, despite the paradox: that is, a completely fallacious doctrine (Descombes concurring) — "is made up of [two] ideas," Descombes says,

---

16 It's important to remember that Descartes was trying to meet seventeenth-century objections, not those of our own time. For a sense of how he may have viewed Princess Elisabeth's questions (and why his options seem so unpromising to us), see the clever (but alien) suggestions offered Descartes in Daniel Garber, 'Understanding Interaction: What Descartes Should Have Told Elisabeth', *The Southern Journal of Philosophy*, 21 (1983), pp. 15–32. I owe the reference to a Polish colleague, Aleksandra Łukaszewicz Alcaraz. (I confess that when I first heard of Garber's paper, I thought it was a joke.)

on the one hand, the individual is all there is (society is thus nothing but a collection of individuals); yet, on the other hand, the society that we form when confronted with other societies is the nation (meaning that it is not the village or the clan, etc.), and the reality of the nation is expressed by the fact that it presents itself, with regard to other nations, as a political individual.[17]

But Descombes *loses* the indispensable fact that, sharing meanings among natural languages must be described in collective terms. We must be clear about what we've agreed to. *Descombes* means to *defend* the reality of "holist" or (let us say) "collective" entities; though he apparently does not realize that his would-be defense forfeits the acknowledgement of events and facts that *require the admission of the collective thought and behavior of the aggregated members of every human society.* So he's made no progress. My own view is that we must allow the presence of *collective features* among the *aggregated* speech and thought and action of the constituent individual persons of the societies in question. Nothing else will do. A "nation," we must say, *is* (if we admit its actuality at all) a "collective individual" somehow comprising what we otherwise count as an aggregate of individual persons, now treated *as* constituent "parts" (in some politically pertinent sense) of the putative collective individual (the people or "nation") — speaking in the mongrel way.

Let me now, in bringing the argument to a close, confess that I have a better answer to our puzzle, that confronts Descombes straight on. I have no intention of abandoning the mongrel liberty, however: it "saves the phenomena" we must describe and explain — where our conceptual and verbal resources still fail us; but it discloses an important mistake on Wittgenstein's part and, in the bargain, discloses the flexibility of the pragmatist's instrumentalist and minimalist bent regarding the puzzles of First Philosophy. In confronting the principal forms of rationalism, therefore, pragmatism owes us an ampler account of its own philosophical competence, where it insists on the transience and inseparability of experience and thought; rejects every form of apriorist, essentialist, necessitarian arguments; concedes the inconstant, diverse, fragmented, historied, uncertain, passing, impressionable, contested, distorted, biased, partial, incompatible, constructed, assuredly never foundational, cognitively qualified disclosures on which we must rely. We say we aim at resolutions that are "as good as we need"; but that's a promissory note that must be redeemed. Here, we need only settle the local contest.

---

17   Descombes, *The Institutions of Meaning*, p. 127n8.

I take the mastery of natural language to be the very paradigm of a collective practice, in the straightforward sense in which, although speech, as a form of action, is normally ascribed to individual persons (even when they are agents of collective entities), the *meanings* of what we say, construed as objectively confirmable in some consensual way among apt speakers, *is* collectively defined — in the sense of belonging to an aggregation of apt speakers who share a "form of life" (a *Lebensform*), that no one actually invents or controls or can ever know completely or authoritatively. We speak a common language (though we speak it in idiosyncratically diverse ways) in the sense in which we acquire our mastery by similar forms of linguistic and cultural immersion and because we acknowledge in an incompletely explicit way that the apparent norms of our linguistic practice are embedded in the practice itself. The tale may be extended indefinitely.

The decisive "collective" factor is simply this: that our aggregated speech and action manifest what we deem to be the *collective attributes* of our shared language. Since, however, as I've already argued, selves or persons are the artifactual transforms of human primates, produced by mastering a natural language, we ourselves exhibit (what may be rightly regarded as) collectively uniform capacities answering to the collective regularities of speech itself. (The distinction is *predicative* rather than individuative.) In that way, as Peirce affirms (but does not adequately pursue), *we* "are" — we become — the mongrel "parts" of a collectively characterized form of life. But to say *that* is merely to nominalize (for convenience *and* effect) the intimacy of our sharing, individually, such potent cultural regularities! All of Descombes's contradictions and incoherencies suddenly fall away. We *are*, mongrelly, "parts" of a "collective individual" in that our speech (and all that that makes possible) manifests certain inescapably collective properties.

To speak here of individual selves as "parts" of a collective individual (a people or nation, say) remains a mongrel liberty all right (now made thoroughly benign, since we now can claim to possess an adequate, pertinent, self-consistent explanation of the collective factor wanted; but then it was already benign in the mongrel way when we lacked the obvious solution — even if we could never have hit on the enabling clue. The relevance of the mongrel functionality of ordinary discourse for the further fortunes of pragmatism rests with the fact that, with the stalemate of rationalist and apriorist presumptions, pragmatism is led to see the argumentative advantages of abandoning hostages to privileged philosophical solutions of any kind.

I'm prepared to guess that professional philosophy will be bound to turn in an increasingly minimalist or instrumentalist direction. I find the tendency distinctly compromised — confusedly — by the Pittsburghers. Nevertheless, according to the evidence I've been assembling regarding the deeper uncertainties of Kantian and Fregean rationalism, it's more than likely that the late-blooming rationalist ardors of our day — largely Fregean in Brandom's efforts (though too optimistic when applied to the natural sciences and in practical contexts), and largely Kantian in McDowell's labors (but much too arbitrary in the necessitarian way when applied naturalistically to the experienced world) — will lead to an even deeper reversal in favor of pragmatism. That is, when the rigors of rationalism are suitably stalemated. I end, therefore, on a modestly prophetic note. I'm persuaded that experience and thought cannot be disjoined in any account of the capacities of human persons; and that the grounds for stalemating both Kantian and Fregean rationalism have been adequately noted in these lectures, though admittedly not in a sufficiently explicit form. My purpose, however, has been to define what I now regard as pragmatism's best philosophical options for the near future.

There remains, however, a final by-benefit to acknowledge. The mongrel functionality of ordinary discourse can claim, and wishes to claim, no necessities or universalities of its own: effectively, it's the natural opponent of Kantian transcendental (and Fregean rationalist) claims. It therefore challenges transcendentalism's would-be explicative powers in at least two important ways: for one thing, it exposes the fact that Kant nowhere specifies or legitimates the rational provenance of the transcendental idiom itself — hence, nowhere vouchsafes its logical or functional difference from the vocabularies of ordinary discourse and conjectured or confirmed explanations (theoretical, nomological, predictive, systematic) among any and all *bona fide* sciences; accordingly, for another, it cannot fail to afford a perfectly plausible, intractably opposed, alternative reading of the would-be *logical* powers of transcendental inquiry itself — that is, as yielding no more than mongrel liberties of its own or as merely failing to secure its claim to engage synthetic *a priori* truths. In this sense, the fortunes of pragmatism and rationalism are ineluctably entwined. My intuition is that this is a variant of what may well have to be the most strategically placed contest of contemporary philosophy.

NORMS *MISJUDGED*
(The Michael Eldridge Lecture)

I

Self-styled "Kantians" tend to believe they can confer with one another amicably, as Kantians, in a de-transcendentalized world. They claim to have salvaged some worthy and viable remnant of the rationalist powers of Kant's original Critical venture, even as they avoid invoking any of the excessive apriorisms noisily ascribed the method of the first *Critique*, I confess I more than doubt the rigor of their zeal, but it sets them, unmistakably, apart. The most extreme version of this form of play is already incipient in the surmise (ours, let us suppose) that Kant himself was, from time to time, actually at work, at naturalizing, in the pages of the first *Critique*, his own picture of the apriorist powers of the understanding on which he constructs his Critical theory. There is some seeming evidence that the conjecture may be true. I don't mean by that that the epistemology of the first *Critique* could possibly survive, de-transcendentalized; only that Kant must have contemplated some moderate conceptual surgery that might, in time — well, perhaps, in our time — have amounted to an effectively de-transcendentalizing maneuver anyway. Those, however, understandably dubious about Peter Strawson's radical recommendation (but convinced nevertheless of the need for some sort of heroic intervention) never quite explain the pertinence and validity of the continuum of cognitive powers deriving from Kant's apriorist presumptions down to our own naturalized or de-transcendenalized replacements, always reasonably proposed (we're assured), within the bounds of a recuperated Critical practice. Here, I think of figures of special interest in our time, figures remarkably influenced by Kant, ranging over theoretical and practical matters alike, figures including Ernst Cassirer, C.I. Lewis, Peter Strawson, Wilfrid Sellars, Jürgen Habermas, John McDowell, Karl-Otto Apel, John Rawls, Christine Korsgaard, and even Charles Peirce and Michel Foucault, to name a small number closest to the purposes of my own remarks — which I admit are a tad subversive.

I think we *can* find some promising evidence of this sort of temptation — for instance, the deep revision of Kant's Critical system, rather brilliantly sustained, applied to the history of physics, in the closing pages of Ernst Cassirer's *Philosophy of Symbolic Forms*, with explicit attribution to Kant's original texts; hence, then, also, in the companionable passages of Kant's first *Critique* — under the heading, "Appendix to the transcendental dialectic," which Kant inserts (completely deadpan) more in the manner of an improved phrasing than of a deep correction of what had appeared to be the triumphal doctrine of the Introductions to both editions of the first *Critique*.[1] Cassirer's gloss shows the way to capturing the would-be rationalist promise of Kant's boldest economy (in the first *Critique*), approaching a "naturalistic" reading of his own "transcendental" resources. Here, Cassirer's emendation (as I read it and as I guess at Kant's ulterior concern in the Appendix), *Vernunft* seems on the point of advising *Verstand* about the evolving possibilities of apperceptive unity and their effect on the accommodating use of "constitutive" and "regulative" conjectures among the restless physical sciences:

> Here [Cassirer affirms, closing the third volume of *Symbolic Forms* with Kant's own words] we are dealing with a genuine transcendental idea in the Kantian sense, and no definite individual experience can accord with it. But to this idea [that is, the idea of abandoning all strictly "constitutive" principles or of construing them as ineluctably contingent] we shall also have to impute an "admirable and necessary regulative use," namely, "as regulative ideas, directing the understanding to a certain aim, the guiding lines towards which all its laws follow, and in which they shall meet in one poin. This point — though a mere idea (*focus imaginarius*), that is, not a point from which the conceptions of the understanding do really proceed, for it lies beyond the sphere of possible experience — serves notwithstanding to give to these conceptions the greatest possible unity combined with the greatest possible extension".[2]

I take this to be the shadow of an extraordinary hint on Kant's part, applied then to the history of physics, and thus duplicated and extended by Cassirer himself, successful only in the relaxed sense that we refuse to look too closely at the revisions of the original transcendental practice

---

1   See Ernst Cassirer, *The Philosophy of Symbolic Forms*, vol. 3, trans. Ralph Manheim (New Haven: Yale University Press, 1957), pp. 475–479. The "Appendix to the Transcendental Dialectic," in the first *Critique*, appears at A642/B670–A704/B732: the operative passage (which Cassirer cites) appears at A643/B671–A645/B673.

2   Cassirer, *The Philosophy of Symbolic Forms*, p. 478

required by both Kant and Cassirer. For how could Kant — or anyone — possibly know that his *a priori* guesses would accurately anticipate the empirical and seemingly systematic corrections of a historied physics? I add only the minor finding (if that is what it is) that the changes wrought completely obviate the need for Kant's insistence on the strict necessity and universality of would-be transcendental truths: "transcendental ideas [Kant finally says, speaking of *Vernunft*] are never of constitutive use... they are merely sophistical [there]".[3] Extraordinary insistence on Kant's part, given Cassirer's accommodation of the actual demands of physics, which, in my opinion, completely betrays the uneasy thesis of Kant's Critical method in both theoretical and practical contexts; *and*, if there, then also, I surmise, possibly by conceptual infection, in all the regressive revivals of rationalism — Cartesian, Kantian, Fregean, Carnapian, Frankfurt Critical, Pittsburgher — especially in the twentieth and twenty-first centuries. There might be no disjunction between *Verstand* and *Vernunft*; *Vernunft* might claim to have found a necessary meta-condition on the constitutive constraints of *Verstand*; in fact, following Cassirer's proposal, *Vernunft* might rightly claim that, necessarily, no synthetic regulative constraint on *Verstand*'s objective yield could possibly obtain without returning Kant to the very rationalisms he was combating.

I don't deny that Kant (and Cassirer and any other aspiring Kantians of our time) — for instance, the John McDowell of the second Woodbridge lecture — are perfectly entitled to claim to have recovered the "regulative use" of a would-be transcendental idea of what a physical or natural "object" must be like; but that usage could no longer claim to serve (in Kant's sense) "an excellent and indispensable necessary regulative use",[4] along the lines just barely broached. In our own time, it happens to be no longer clear what a physical "object" must be like! Ultimately, Kant offers no further transcendental clue that undoes the potential mischief of the passage I've cited from the "Appendix to the Transcendental Dialectic"; Kant freely acknowledges that his speculation exceeds all possible experience. Bear that in mind, please; it may be fairly read as signifying that it violates the essential constraint of all of Kant's transcendental resources, places Kant squarely among the admirable rationalists of the seventeenth and eighteenth centuries that he himself means to combat. Failure here, I dare suggest,

---

3   Immanuel Kant, *Critique of Pure Reason*, trans. Paul Guyer and Allen W. Wood (Cambridge: Cambridge University Press, 1998), A644/B672.
4   Kant, *Critique of Pure Reason*, A624/B642. See John McDowell, *The Logical Form of an Intention*, in *Having the World in View: Essays on Kant, Hegel, and Sellars* (Cambridge: Harvard University Press, 2009), pp. 23–43.

may be prophecy enough of the likely failure of the bolder (rationalist) successors of the nineteenth, twentieth, and early twenty-first centuries. In any event, *what* is the advantage of rejecting noumenalism but coddling the "necessities" of transcendentalism, naturalized or not? The putative advantage — and its plausibility — escape me.

In any event: yield on the "constitutive" principle, I say, and you must yield on the "regulative" principle as well. (There would be nothing to regulate if there were nothing strictly constituted.) Accordingly, one *could* say that the transcendental had been de-transcendentalized, even naturalized or defeated, by Cassirer's demonstrating that reason must be accorded substantive powers over understanding — but then only at the cost of there no longer being any vestige of apriorist necessity (regarding, say, the "Intentionality" of physical objects or the conceptual fixity of what a "physical object" must be like) to conjure with. And if that proved true, there would be no pertinent reason, *a priori* or otherwise, to hold to any part of Kant's argument in favor of empirical realism. Kant would stand before us as no more than a notably ingenious rationalist or dogmatist of precisely the sort he was himself combating. In that case, Charles Peirce's extraordinarily prescient verdict — namely, that "Kant (whom [as Peirce says] I *more* than admire) is nothing but a somewhat confused pragmatist"[5] — would be itself instantly and completely vindicated. Peirce, I should add, clearly takes Kant to have treated the *Ding-an-sich* illicitly — in cognitive terms.

I've now introduced, obliquely, for my present purpose, the utter vulnerability of Kant's notion of transcendental necessity. I say that Kant without the transcendental necessity of synthetic *a priori* truths is hardly the true Kant *and* that the transcendental reading of the conditions of realism in the sciences would have to be abandoned by Kant himself; furthermore, that what's true for the transcendental treatment of scientific claims can hardly fail to be matched among practical claims — which, on Kant's account, as with moral issues, though they cannot be treated strictly as truth-claims, must nevertheless remain at least rationally valid.

But if so, then, inasmuch as Kant believes he can secure the necessity and universal applicability of the regulative principle of reason (applied in both theoretical and practical contexts), *to* be obliged (at least implicitly, on Cassirer's evidence from the history of physics) to give up the putative

---

5   Charles Peirce, Collected Papers of Charles Sanders Peirce, vol. 5, eds. Charles Hartshorne and Paul Weiss (Cambridge: Harvard University Press, 1934, 1962), 5.525.

necessity and universal scope of the very concept of a "law of nature" would
be to lose as well the supposedly secure practical analogy of acting "as if"
our maxims of rational entitlement could still be read (as Kant requires) as
self-promulgated laws of nature. Of course, Kant's reasoning about human
autonomy and the categorical imperative is a gymnastic marvel of its own
— but never mind. The apparent arbitrariness, the possible irrelevance,
the dubious meaning of a universalistic criterion of maxims of conduct is
difficult to dispel.

Hence, if it proved true that, as in the notably robust pragmatist analysis
of physical laws advanced by Nancy Cartwright (favored as well by an
impressive number of like-minded commentators of every persuasion,
from Otto Neurath to Richard Feynman to Bas van Fraassen), *to* treat the
regularities of empirical research in the physical sciences as if they were,
necessarily, asymptotic instantiations of the transcendental conditions of
a true law of nature would simply be to falsify the actual state of play in
contemporary physics; for, according to Cartwright, a conceptual analysis
of scientific practices effectively confirms *that* "the laws of physics [do
indeed] lie," which is in fact the explicit lesson Cartwright draws from
the very first sentence of her book (which yields its title as her charge):
"Philosophers [she begins] distinguish phenomenological from theoretical
laws".[6] In effect, she draws attention to the *empirical* vulnerability of
would-be transcendental reasoning and the "idealized" deformation of
scientific data.

Insistence on the strict necessity of the would-be formal properties of
the explanatory laws of nature might then produce an even greater scandal
in the world of human freedom and autonomy. For, then, it would turn out
that the acknowledged conditions of moral conduct (in Kant's account)
would be completely satisfied merely and only by adhering to no more
than the contrived universality of whatever principles the validity of our
agentive "maxims" claimed to favor.

Of course, that would be an intolerable state of affairs: first, because the
putative necessity of the formal conditions of autonomous rational behavior
would be falsified by the confirmed practices of the sciences themselves;
second, because, as Hegel rightly argues and as the infamous *Reichstag* fire
episode confirms, nearly any maxim for acting rationally can be tricked out
in universalist form, without anyone's being persuaded that the practice
was valid because the trick was turned; third, because, if that's true, then,

---

6   See Nancy Cartwright, *How the Laws of Physics Lie* (Oxford: Clarendon, 1983),
       p. 1.

abandoning the constraint of the categorical imperative, there would no longer be any rationalist conditions of Kant's sort by which to govern moral behavior; and, fourth, because at least some contemporary philosophers close to Kant — Christine Korsgaard for one — actually believe that the merely formal constraint *is* indeed the only ("regulative") principle Kant requires. I shall, shortly, draw your attention to some revealing comparisons (within the practical sphere) involving the pronouncements of John Rawls and Jürgen Habermas — the leading Kantian-inclined moral-political philosophers of the twentieth century. I'm hinting, here, I should say, at the massive vulnerability of the late revival of Kantian rationalism in moral-political matters. (I would have added: of Fregean rationalism as well, but I cannot do justice to that extension here.) Nevertheless, I do want to alert you, however briefly, to the heightened presence (in our own time) of a grander contest regarding the revival of rationalist philosophies, which I touch on obliquely — perhaps, not negligibly.

Christine Korsgaard, in fact, is more than ordinarily resourceful in defending her version of a Kantian theory of moral rectitude; also, apart from its own possibilities, her actual account captures an essential theme of the original motivation of the very different Kantian-like ventures pursued by Rawls and Habermas, both of whom are very nearly forced to abandon anything akin to Kant's rationalist vision of an ideal moral world — or else they continue, most improbably, to support discrete elements of Kant's (abstract) vision, in the face of conceptual difficulties that arise among individualistic moral theories confronted by the collective and communal practices of historied societies. These difficulties, which affect the very notion of what it is to be an autonomous moral agent, are now often dubbed "ethical" concerns, to distinguish them from issues regarding "moral" or Kantian universalist principles — partly in accord with a suggestion advanced by Bernard Williams.[7] But Williams's suggestion broaches important difficulties that cannot be rightly captured by mere instrumental or liberal considerations (a charge Williams finds contemporary Kantian moralists consistently fail to grasp).

Rawls, I surmise, became painfully aware of the problematic status of the universalist claims of *A Theory of Justice*, said to be rationally vindicated *only behind* "the veil of ignorance." Accordingly, Rawls falls back — I would say, correctly, though much too slowly and without

---

7   See, for instance, Bernard Williams, *Morality, the Peculiar Institution*, in *Ethics and the Limits of Philosophy* (Cambridge: Harvard University Press, 1985), pp. 184–196. Williams recommends we abandon the "moral."

adequate explanation, in *Political Liberalism* (1993, 1996) and *The Law of Peoples* (1999) — to rereading his own would-be legitimated *moral* theory as (conceivably) little more than a genuinely attractive reformulation of a liberal ideology.[8] That's to say: Rawls had to have realized that *Political Liberalism* was *not* primarily an ideology conveniently abstracted from a prior moral theory that he *had* already successfully *shown* to be objectively valid, but (instead) a fallback position forced upon him by his own argument — effectively, the ideological nerve *of A Theory of Justice* itself; hence, then, also, that *The Law of Peoples* was never the extension of any domestic moral theory within the scope of *A Theory of Justice*, applied to international matters, but only the extension of the liberal ideology of *A Theory of Justice* itself, applied to those same questions. Rawls was aware that mere domestic solutions could not be validly applied in international contexts involving states and peoples, if, say, cosmopolitanism (and methodological individualism) could not be satisfactorily validated as well. Rawls's discovery of his own conversion of a liberal ideology into a universal moral theory led him inexorably to the *non*-liberal requirements of his unfinished last reflections.

The shock of discovery seems to have been more than ordinarily troubling for Rawls: we cannot be sure, even now, just how much of his original theory unravels under these charges. I suspect it must be the entire theory, since it's meant to be both objectively valid and foundational in Rawls's "domestic" setting. The question haunts Rawls's entire undertaking: certainly, it's unreasonable to suppose that an improved liberal individualism is either demonstrably valid or the best — or included among the best — rational(ist) moral theories that we could possibly advance (that is, domestically or generalized over contemporary democracies). Rawls never completed the deep revisions he himself came to see would be required of his *Theory of Justice* — the gist of which may be summarized in terms of the need to reject the cosmopolitan option, bare liberalism itself, and, very possibly, if we admit historical change and evolution, the very defensibility of *any* ideally universalized "foundation" of morality — which, in different ways, both Habermas and Korsgaard favor.

I'm persuaded that Habermas and Korsgaard fail to see (at least in good part) what Rawls came to construe as a decisive threat to the essential premises of his original proposal — just where he lacked time enough to

---

8   See John Rawls, *Political Liberalism*, revised (New York: Columbia University Press, 1993, 1996); and *The Law of Peoples*, with "The Idea of Public Reason Revisited" (Cambridge: Harvard University Press, 1999).

address the matter effectively. Rawls simply outstripped liberalism and his own liberal theory of justice. He was aware that his fledgling account of "peoples" remained inchoate but would, in time, triumph (ineluctably) over liberalism itself. He also grasped the essential paradox of attempting to reconcile the primacy of persons and the requirements of collective or communal "entities" — including the *aporia* of defining such entities ("peoples," as he named them), in accord with the requirements of global justice.

In this sense, I dare suggest, Rawls is, finally, more instructive than Kant, though largely because Kant was willing to test the limits of his own impossible proposal. Ultimately, rationalism, in the practical sphere, is conceptually hopeless: it can never regularize history convincingly. But then, apart from arithmetic and (perhaps) some few related disciplines, rationalism applied to theoretical matters (whether in Kantian or Fregean guise) stands defeated as an autonomous cognitive faculty. (This is itself a huge topic that I address elsewhere as an entirely independent question.) In any case, for those sorts of reasons, Rawls's theory is much more important than either Habermas's or Korsgaard's.

Rawls, let me add, was aware, finally, that his original theory of justice was hardly more than the barest *fragment*, even intuitively, of the normative structure of a "basic" domestic democracy: first, because Rawls nowhere examines the sense in which his liberal premise applies to a *people*, any people (or, a nation or a state), or to how the lacuna might affect the concept of justice itself; second, because, as he himself says, he does not know how the relationship between a specimen people and "a society of peoples" is likely to affect the validity of any would-be domestic model of justice applied to peoples that live with very different practices and different conceptions of the relationship that holds between individuals and their encompassing "peoples"; and, third, because human societies are continually evolving, historically, in diverse and novel and unexpected ways that cannot possibly vouchsafe any meaningful approximation to the ahistorical universalities with which Rawls himself begins his originally confident speculation.

Is there any validity at all in such an approach? The question belongs to Rawls's late reflections on the naïve guesses of his original vision: *not*, mind you, guesses about his own moral ideology but about what, arguably, *is* universally valid in liberalism itself. He's put the abstract universalism of rationalist moralities at mortal risk — and he knows it. He's aware he's backed into Hegel's quarrel with Kant. There's nobility there, to be sure, but there's also nonsense and a great deal of lost time. The irony is that

Rawls has gone (unwillingly) beyond himself and well beyond Kant. He's turned away from Kant's "moral" principles toward so-called "ethical" concerns — perhaps, a narrowed sliver of Hegel's "*Sittlichkeit*" — possibly prompted by Bernard Williams's knowledgeable salute to Hegel, even as Williams (perhaps also Rawls) grasped the need to go beyond the merely disjunctive options offered. "The purest Kantian view [says Williams, already in 1985, having Rawls in mind] locates the importance of morality in the importance of moral motivation itself.... This view was relentlessly and correctly attacked by Hegel, on the grounds that it gave moral thought no content." In the Preface to *Ethics and the Limits of Philosophy* (in which the line just cited appears), Williams issues his own conclusion before his argument:

> the demands of the modern world on ethical thought [he says] are unprecedented, and the ideas of rationality embodied in most contemporary moral philosophy [read here: "Rawls's moral philosophy"] cannot meet them; but some extension of ancient thought, greatly modified [read here: "Aristotle's ethics"] might be able to do so.[9]

I'm persuaded that Rawls was chagrined to discover that, without grasping the full import of his own brief, he'd retraced a decisive but forgotten quarrel, under the innocent history of nearly fifty years since the publication of *A Theory of Justice*; he saw something of *its* import for our own future. But he himself was not allotted time enough to turn his hand to answering its revived challenge — nor was it adequately grasped, apparently, by any other skilled "Kantian" of our day. The point is, if the argument holds true, then Rawls's unexpected contribution *is*, precisely, to have defeated himself in the simplest possible way and, because of that, to have led the way to reversing the entire direction of Western moral philosophy — away from Kantian morality back to the contingencies of ethical practice — hence, then, to the unassailable informality of philosophical rigor that concedes the inseparability of ideology and objectivity. That was hardly Rawls's original intent. But, of course, it's Rawls's own authority that stands behind his candor. He was an original champion of a return to Kantian inspiration and, finally, as it turned out, an incipiently deeper critic of the problematic universalism of Kant's liberal vision. There can be no principled separation between reason and experience in the human world.

---

9   Bernard Williams, *Ethics and the Limits of Philosophy*, (Cambridge: Harvard University Press, 1985), pp. 184, vii.

II

Habermas does not go as far as Rawls (in going beyond Kant), in contesting the primacy of his own Kantian thesis: his "discourse ethics." But then, he never succeeded in reconciling the would-be naturalized transcendentalism of the discourse theory and his would-be pragmatist treatment of rational consensus, both of which he's pursued through his entire career — in spite of the fact that he addresses the actual problems of "peoples" (nations and states) of contemporary Europe.[10] There's no question that Habermas's "discourse ethics" is a primitive contrivance, much as Kant's categorical imperative is, possibly a vestige of his long association with Karl-Otto Apel, who (for his part) found Kant altogether *too lax* in his own transcendental efforts![11] The question haunts the whole of Habermas's venture. I don't believe it can be resolved along universalist lines and (*pace* Kant) I don't see why it should be thought to require, or gain strength from, any such formal constraint. (In any event, Habermas's rationalism was never more than doubtfully secured.) The upshot is that, for all of his labors, Habermas's liberal-democratic intransigence seems more arbitrary than Rawls's deeply felt dissatisfaction with liberal theory. The reason (I conjecture) is simply that Rawls, at the end of his life, found himself drawn to challenging all the signs of Western hegemony; whereas Habermas seems to have been unassailably committed to his rationalist vision, all the while he searched for the elusive ingenuities of a "feasible utopia."

I can now pinpoint Rawls's unresolved difficulty, by drawing on the summary reviews (and revisions) succinctly provided in his final book, *Justice as Fairness*, which catches up and eclipses the main lines of *A Theory of Justice*. I daresay the principal lines of what Rawls would have

---

10   See, for instance, the difference between Jürgen Habermas, *Discourse Ethics: Notes on a Program of Philosophical Justification*, in *Moral Consciousness and Communicative Action*, trans. Christian Lenhardt and Shierry Weber Nicholsen (Cambridge: MIT Press, 1990), pp. 43–115; and Jürgen Habermas, *Between Facts and Norms: Contributions to a Discourse Theory of Law and Democracy*, trans. William Rehg (Cambridge: MIT Press, 1996).

11   See, for instance Apel's extraordinary proposals, in Karl-Otto Apel, *Transcendental semiotics and the paradigms of First Philosophy*, in *From a transcendental-semiotic point of view*, ed. Marianna Papastephanou (Manchester: Manchester University Press, 1998), pp. 43–63; and *The a priori of the communication community and the foundations of ethics: the problem of a rational foundation of ethics and a scientific age*, in *Towards a Transformation of Philosophy*, trans. Glyn Adey and David Frisby (London: Routledge & Kegan Paul, 1980), p. 277.

fleshed out, had he survived a few more years, are neatly collected in the following few lines from *Justice as Fairness*:

> A... limit of our inquiry [Rawls acknowledges] is that we shall not here discuss the important question of the just relations between peoples, nor how the extension of justice as fairness to these relations illustrates the way in which it is suitably universal... A just world order is perhaps best seen as a society of peoples, each people maintaining a well-ordered and decent political (domestic) regime, not necessarily democratic but fully respecting basic human rights... In justice as fairness, the question of justice between peoples is postponed until we have an account of political justice for a well-ordered democratic society. Observe, though, that beginning with the justice of the basic structure does not imply that we cannot revise our account for a democratic society (domestic justice) in view of what justice between peoples turns out to require.[12]

That final sentence — the one just cited — puts in mortal jeopardy all the brave words that precede it: Rawls begins to sound like a more uncertain witness within the contest contrived by Habermas and Foucault.

The decisive fact to remark here is that Rawls was aware of the profound incompleteness of his theory of justice, given that the liberal conception he begins with (in *A Theory of Justice*), which he effectively takes to be both "rationally" and "reasonably" universal, as well as foundational, itself *depends* (in some as yet unexplained way) on the requirements of the integral identity of *"peoples."* If you see that, you cannot fail to see Rawls's utter dissatisfaction with his own misprision of the *ideological* limitations of *A Theory of Justice*. International (or global) justice apparently requires some form of respect for the collective forms of life of different peoples, *that cannot be captured by any universal liberal-democratic formula* and yet affects the validity of any such formula. But, of course, if that's true, then Rawls is no longer restricted to liberal-democratic values. Ponder that!

Now, if we turn to Habermas and Korsgaard, we find very little in their texts that might contribute in any way to lifting Rawls's self-imposed stalemate. This is particularly surprising in Habermas's case: Habermas, it seems, was unable to surpass the *aporia* of his commitment to the pragmatism of consensus and the de-transcendentalized necessity of his "discourse ethics." Korsgaard remains remarkably steadfast as a Kantian, by comparison with Rawls (who was, of course, her teacher) and also when compared with Habermas. The reason must be that she finds the abstract formula of the categorical imperative entirely adequate when appropriately

---

12   John Rawls, *Justice as Fairness: A Restatement*, ed. Erin Kelly (Cambridge: Harvard University Press, 2001), pp. 13–14 (§5.1).

incorporated into her reading of Kant's notion of the "Kingdom of Ends." She clearly believes that the "Kingdom" *is* a feasible objective *in* the world we actually inhabit: it's a feasible utopia (as Rawls might have said in another context); in fact, Korsgaard *is* indeed a benign but severe cosmopolitan. Habermas is also a cosmopolitan, though that may strike you as unlikely. In any case, it begins to explain why Rawls finds no late Kantian-like discovery involving a concern for peoples that might have informed his earlier theory of justice.

Turn back to Habermas again. In a well-known paper on the future of a united Europe (1991) Habermas concludes a notably sanguine appraisal of Europe's current prospects (well before the onset of the Syrian and Middle Eastern and African refugee problem, of course) with the following revealing verdict, which (I daresay) betrays Habermas's having completely misunderstood the import of both his and Rawls's discussions of the complexities of international and global moral-political concerns — which cannot possibly be rendered in terms of liberal-capitalist or liberal-democratic, or Lockean, or methodologically individualistic, or (generally) Western conceptions of citizenship:

> Within the constitutional framework of the democratic rule of law [Habermas affirms] diverse forms of life can coexist equally. These must, however, overlap in a common political culture that in turn is open to impulses from new forms of life.
>
> Only a democratic citizenship that does not close itself off in a particularistic fashion can pave the way for a *world citizenship*, which is already taking shape in worldwide political communications. The Vietnam War, the revolutionary changes in eastern and central Europe, as well as the Gulf War, are the first *world-political* events in the strict sense.[13]

Habermas's mistake, here, lies with his supposing that a politically united Europe is a linearly progressive *step* in the direction of world government or "world citizenship" of a kind fundamentally different from what Nancy Fraser has labeled "the Westphalian" or "Keynesian-Westphalian frame" (of sovereign states). There's no question that Europe had, for some time, been witnessing a fading or thinning of national boundaries and an interest in a united Europe (a trend now definitely reversed, with the onset of the Syrian wars, Russian and Chinese and American adventures, and the rise

---

13   Jürgen Habermas, Appendix 2: "Citizenship and National Identity" (1990) in *Between Facts and Norms: Contributions to a Discourse Theory of Law and Democracy*, trans. William Rehg (Cambridge: MIT Press, 1996), pp. 491–515, citation at p. 514.

of ISIS and similar non-state powers). The outcome of recent European developments, *vis-à-vis* Habermas's prediction, has still to be properly assessed. But even if some sort of political union were to take form in Europe, it's likely to be a *mélange* of different sorts of collectivity that continue to favor *some* realistic form of sovereignty at the top; so that it is not likely to be a step *toward* "world citizenship" in Habermas's sense. *That's not what is happening*!

I doubt that anything of Habermas's kind of liberalism will develop for at least another thousand years, unless, of course, the Martians are more advanced and more fearsome than we suppose. No doubt, what Nancy Fraser calls the "Keynesian-Westphalian frame" *is* morphing into something concerned with new forms of monetary, manufacturing, trading, and allied technological activities. But I see no evidence that the trend is moving (or will move) in the direction of world citizenship. It is, perhaps, signaling the onset and development of cleverer forms of world capitalism, which have indeed already (and for some time) begun to breach the regulative capacities of nearly all national states.[14]

The most acute and accurate analysis of what we may respectfully call the Kantian — or perhaps, better, the neo-meta-, neo-neo-Kantian conceptual crisis (otherwise, the utter confusion of contemporary moral as well as epistemological rationalism) — appears in a few lines by Michael Kelly, attempting to capture the threatening incoherence of the contrived confrontation between Habermas and Foucault: that's to say, the confrontation that never took place but is nevertheless recorded in Kelly's edited collection, *Critique and Power*, drawing on publications by Habermas and Foucault and others. Kelly captures the impassable stalemate, beginning with a line from Habermas:

> 'The transcendental moment of *universal* validity [he cites Habermas as affirming] bursts every provinciality asunder.' The presuppositions of modernity [Kelly then adds] are historical in origin, our reconstructions of them are fallible, yet their validity is transcendent. This is also true of modernity as a whole; although it arose only a few hundred years ago, it is not merely one of many historical traditions which we can voluntarily adopt or discard;

---

14   See Nancy Fraser, *Scales of Justice: Reimagining Political Space in a Globalizing World* (New York: Columbia University Press, 2009), Chs. 3–4. It's possible that Habermas's commitment to his universalized "discourse ethic" (which is itself problematic) might have suggested to him a "matching" tendency toward "world citizenship" (effectively, also universalized). But that seems (to me) like self-deception. My own guess is that we are already deeply involved with totalitarian tendencies that are not directed by individual or cooperating states.

modernity, too, is universal and thus irreversible, intractable, unavoidable...
According to Foucault, the transcendence Habermas speaks of is not something
about which we could ever have any epistemological assurance so long as our
reason is historical.[15]

Confronted with his own impasse, Rawls respectfully yields ground, but
dies before he is able to answer fairly; Habermas's courage obliged him
to make the transcendental completely ineffable, prophetic, outflanking
Karl-Otto Apel's scolding; and Korsgaard remains utterly serene in the
utopian adequacy of a de-transcendentalized categorical imperative. Of
course, Kant's transcendentalism is itself collected as a promising instance
of Habermas's transcendent transcendentalism.

The leading Kantian moralists of our day fall short of providing the
conceptual resources (we discover are) needed for a thorough analysis
of any would-be basic and viable liberal morality: that is, regarding
the adequacy of methodological individualism itself and the obscure
relationship between an individualistic morality (itself already in internal
tension regarding political and public but non-political interests) and the
similarly divided interests and moralities of collective "bodies" (states
or nations or "peoples," as in Rawls's improved analytic vocabulary),
pertinently effective and engaged at every level of significant human life
— notably neglected in the would-be liberalism of *A Theory of Justice*
but inventively recovered, however slowly and with whatever uncertainty,
in *Political Liberalism* and *The Law of Peoples*. Rawls is the best of the
liberalist lot, if for no other reason than that he confirms the inherent
inadequacy of Kant's transcendental rationalism and methodological
individualism — and, therefore, the inadequacy of his own variant of a
Kantian-inspired liberalism. He effectively demonstrates that the Kantian
model must be superseded in a number of ways.

It's true that our outlook on the very world we take ourselves to inhabit
has begun to be globalized in historied ways — may, in fact, already be
galactic. Nevertheless, globalization is hardly tantamount to possessing or
contriving any universal or necessary moral principles or any compelling
rationalist ground for same. I, for one, confess I see no reason to insist

---

15   Michael Kelly, *Foucault, Habermas, and the Self-Referentiality of Critique*, in
      Michael Kelly (ed.), *Critique and Power: Recasting the Foucault/Habermas
      Debate* (Cambridge: MIT Press, 1994), pp. 365–400, citation at p. 388. The line
      from Habermas appears in Jürgen Habermas, *The Philosophical Discourse of
      Modernity: Twelve Lectures*, trans. Frederick Lawrence (Cambridge: MIT Press,
      1987), p. 322.

on the primacy (or essentiality) of any such ideal conditions (vestiges, perhaps, of invoking the questionable resources of one or another form of transcendental reason). We have already witnessed, you will recall, the need for Kant to retreat (in the passages of the first *Critique*) from would-be "constitutive" (transcendental) principles and the resultant indeterminacy of "regulative" principles. I also argue, I should add, that as functionally apt persons, we humans are best viewed (on post-Darwinian grounds, attentive to the intertwined biological and cultural evolution and emergence of enlanguaged creatures) as distinctly artifactual, hybrid, historied beings, lacking any essential *telos*, rational or natural, by which to claim or reclaim or validate any would-be necessary or universal norms by which any and every fully agentive life may be rightly and responsibly governed. The result is that, apart from difficulties already remarked, Kant's advocacy of absolute moral norms (for "humanity," say) are, however inspired and noble, simply pulled out of thin air.

There are no synthetic *a priori* rules or laws or principles to be had. There are only the archives of cultural memory and the pronouncements of current human conviction and future hope and reasonable inquiries regarding enabling commitments and the like; and, there, we would have to abandon "pure" obligations and fall back to the contingencies of historical experience and the mundane interests of "ethical" rather than "moral" values, as Bernard Williams suggests, having both Aristotle and Hegel in mind. The categorical imperative is entirely formal and empty (though not without consequences, wherever applied); and, with a minimum of ingenuity, it can always be made compatible with any otherwise self-consistent agentive policy. The transcendental *Ich* is hardly more than a fiction; and the concept of "man as an end, not a means alone" can, again, with a modicum of ingenuity, be made compatible with nearly any self-consistent policy or action.

As far as physical and biological evidence is concerned, the human person has no assignable niche in the world: in any naturalized or de-transcendentalized setting, our moral norms are clearly artifacts of the artifactual human world, *sittlich* (I should say), at least initially, in a modest sense, in accord with the usual transformation or self-transformation of infant primates into enlanguaged persons or apt agents — through the resources of which, (as *gebildet* or "second-natured"), we discover that we are "always already" instructed in the use of the operative norms and practices of our home culture and society. There is, then, always already, a dimension of collective education at work even in the formation of the most restricted liberal interests and convictions.

To admit all this, which I cannot fully legitimate here (but have favored for a longish time), does not signify that morality is a conceptual scam or is incapable of being reasonably advanced or revised — as a "second-best" proposal, that is, as constructed rather than discovered.[16] If you grant all this, you cannot fail to admit the futility of a very large part of Western theories bent on formulating the true boundaries of the moral world. I say, moral and moral-political norms (all agentive norms, for that matter) are committed to the *construction* of at least a *modus vivendi* — consider Hobbes — among aggregated persons and collective peoples, among all the diverse societies of our age. I take that to be the nerve of a pragmatist conception of morality adequate for our time — possibly for any time.

It's also, as I read him, very close to the ultimate target of that would-be arch-liberal — John Rawls — who became aware that mere liberalism, moral rationalism, and any de-transcendentalized or naturalized variant of Kantian universalism (applied to moral and moral-political questions) could never yield a convincing or adequate picture of the moral world: we would remain "ethical" partisans inclined to favor the selection of some adventitious constellation of the practices and values of our own experienced world and would always be aware that, both domestically and internationally, either justice cannot serve as a sufficiently comprehensive human virtue or, where it begins to seem adequate at all, it must supersede (even as it may incorporate) a liberal formulation and begin to center instead on the profound diversity and inequalities (and incommensurabilities) of "peoples" and other collective bodies. It would increasingly feature the neglected relationship between the moral interests of individual and collective agents approaching the boundaries of the global — and more. Rawls persuasively eclipses rationalism, universalism, individualism, liberalism, republicanism, contractarianism, cosmopolitanism, possibly even the assurance that a "reasonable" and "rational" morality can be entirely consistent. It may well be, I conjecture, that morality in the modern world is, logically, a kind of heuristic; although, one way or another, it obviously acquires the force of sanctions.

There is, then, no fundamental difference between a moral ideology and an objective morality, except relativized to our deepest convictions. In that sense, even the reasoned revision of an operative practice is as *sittlich* as any earlier incarnation, in that its "realist" standing rests with its ability

---

16   The most recent version of my view of the required enabling arguments appears in my *Toward a Metaphysics of Culture* (London: Routledge, 2016).

to be validated afresh by consensual support and pertinent considerations. There's danger there, of course; but then, that *is* the human condition. I think here of the hasty and continually changing reception of the refugees now pouring into Europe, confounded by the realities of life itself.

The best we can say is that, relative to survival and some conception of flourishing, we cannot ignore the standard interests and prudential needs of the race (which are at once individual and collective). Admitting that much, there is no assuredly rationalist way to recover any version of the Kantian doctrine or any would-be inviolable moral rule. We are forever at the mercy of ourselves. What we grasp, however — what I'm persuaded Rawls came to realize — is that formalisms of the Kantian sort (his own, for example) risk being completely arbitrary or distorted or irrelevant, though not without consequences (as Korsgaard demonstrates). We cannot *begin*, as Rawls and Habermas and Korsgaard and Kant actually do, with nothing more than the abstract requirement that our motivation must conform with the rational demands of universalism (or quasi-universalism) or transcendental necessities. Every pertinent moral proposal must feature some *contingently* selected constellation of the historied goods and obligations of the *sittlich* world the society we wish to instruct already understands and has in some measure been prepared to support. But that alone ensures the prior contingency and historied bias of any would-be valid moral vision. (I'm persuaded that that must be *part* of the meaning of a Wittgensteinian *Lebensform*, though I also believe that Wittgenstein himself was never a committed historicist.)

Universality, then, is morally unnecessary and unworkable or trivially achieved — contrary to Kant's reading of autonomy — or now, with the benefit of Habermas's *carte blanche*; and if we propose any approximation to bare universality, it would have to be a contingently instrumental, thoroughly subordinate requirement relativized to the partisan resources we claim to favor judiciously. Seen this way, I'm led to believe that Rawls came to realize that he'd reversed the only seemingly viable way of rationally approaching a reasonable proposal for the moral legislation of any part of the population of the world. In that sense, an ideology addressed to so-called ethical goods may be the only way to achieve moral objectivity. But that's to say, with the pragmatists, that there is no fixed priority between moral norms and ethical values. The Kantian procedure is committed to the separability of ideal norms (the formal demand of the categorical imperative) and the relative indifference (at *that* level of reasoning) to what we contingently prefer in the way of the goods and reciprocal benefits we choose to favor.

I've brought the argument to a close that I had already foreseen. It's an outcome that might well claim a sort of comic *pàthos*. It cannot do justice to the Kantian conviction pursued by the liberal Rawls or the cosmopolitan Korsgaard, and it's unwilling to abide by Habermas's rational mystery. You must also bear in mind that Rawls's original liberalism was accessible and defended only under "the veil of ignorance," only "in the original position," and only as eventually contested by Rawls himself. The cosmopolitan endorsement of the categorical imperative is even less promising. Here, for instance, is Korsgaard's literal reading of Kant's principle:

> The categorical imperative [she says] merely tells us to choose a law. Its only constraint on our choice is that it has the form of a law. And nothing determines what the law must be. All that it has to be is a law.[17]

One might well argue that Korsgaard comes very close to matching Habermas's insistence on the transcendental validity of his discourse ethics (independent of the admitted difficulty of approaching any naturalized form of universal rational consensus). "The human will," she says — I take her to be speaking of her own view as well as Kant's — "must be seen as universally legislative".[18] I don't see how such a formulation could not be validly invoked to accommodate ISIL's efforts to construct its caliphate.

Let me, therefore, bring this paper to a proper close. The briefest effective challenge to Korsgaard's proposal that I am aware of appears in Raymond Geuss's rejoinder to the rule just cited, which (that is, the rejoinder) appeared as an invited response to the theory of Korsgaard's *The Sources of Normativity*, in the text itself. Geuss says very simply:

> There should then be some kind of argument to the conclusion that I am essentially a member of the Kingdom of Ends (and only contingently American). Or rather there need to be two arguments: one to convince me that *I* am necessarily a member of a Kingdom of Ends and then another to show the necessary universal extension for this Kingdom of Ends (for me) to *all* other humans.[19]

---

17 A convenient form of Rawls's adjusted argument appears in John Rawls, *The Law of Peoples*, in *On Human Rights: The Oxford Amnesty Lectures*, eds. Stephen Shute and Susan Hurley (New York: Basic Books, 1993), pp. 41–82, 220–30. The citation from Korsgaard is from *The Sources of Normativity*, p. 98.

18 Korsgaard, *Creating the Kingdom of Ends*, p. 23. For a sense of her distinction between "ideal" and "nonideal theory," see pp. 147–154.

19 Raymond Geuss, "Morality and Identity," in *The Sources of Normativity*, pp. 196–197. See, also, Korsgaard, *Creating the Kingdom of Ends*, Ch. 5, especially pp. 151–154. I note here that *Sources* and *Kingdom* were published in the same year.

I see no way of answering without a blatant *petitio*. Here, Geuss rightly mentions the Serbs (in the Kosovo affair) and the Muslim bounty on Salman Rushdie's head; and we, of course, can easily mention the Taliban and ISIL — and ourselves if we are confessionally inclined, under one guise or another. There is, one may rest easy, no failure for believers.

MIMESIS GROUP
www.mimesis-group.com

MIMESIS INTERNATIONAL
www.mimesisinternational.com
info@mimesisinternational.com

MIMESIS EDIZIONI
www.mimesisedizioni.it
mimesis@mimesisedizioni.it

ÉDITIONS MIMÉSIS
www.editionsmimesis.fr
info@editionsmimesis.fr

MIMESIS COMMUNICATION
www.mim-c.net

MIMESIS EU
www.mim-eu.com

Printed by Booksfactory — Szczecin (Poland) in July 2017